The Life of Sr. Mary Wilhelmina

THE LIFE OF SR. MARY WILHELMINA

The Benedictines of Mary, Queen of Apostles

TAN Books
Gastonia, North Carolina

Cover design by www.davidferrisdesign.com

Library of Congress Control Number: 2023941087

ISBN: 978-1-5051-3267-0
Kindle ISBN: 978-1-5051-3269-4
ePUB ISBN: 978-1-5051-3268-7

Published in the United States by
TAN Books
PO Box 269
Gastonia, NC 28053
www.TANBooks.com

Printed in India

"Every man's life is acted out between two great events: his birth and his death. Man has two outlooks: an outlook toward life, and an outlook toward death. The pagan world was, for the most part, oppressed with the outlook toward death. . . .

After centuries of gloom, Christ was born in a poor stable in Bethlehem. This was a birth, which led to a death, which death was to remove the sting and gloom of death forever after from the lives of men. This was the good news, from which the practice of Christianity, a seeming paradox of joy and self-denial, sprang."

—Sister Wilhelmina

Contents

Introduction

"God's will, God's will,
God's will be done!
Praised be the Father,
Praised be the Son!
Praised be Divine Love, Lord Holy Ghost!
Praised be in union with the heavenly host!"

One year after the death of our beloved foundress, the above poem still rings in our ears as though our beloved Sister Wilhelmina were still thumping her cane in time to the unforgettable rhythm of her own creation. This little poem encapsulates her name, her life, her purpose: to show that there is another reality, no less real than what can be perceived around us, that there is indeed a loving God Who seeks only our good, our ultimate happiness, for all eternity.

Sister Wilhelmina understood that true holiness consists not in niceness or pleasant feelings but in a battle of wills; she was determined, at all costs, to surrender her strong will to an even stronger one: the will of God.

It was in the same spirit of the secondary love of her life, the love of her mother, the Blessed Virgin Mary, that she constantly gave her will over to God. In the Blessed Mother, the Word—Our Lord Jesus Christ—became flesh and dwelt among us. In the life of Sister Wilhelmina, a new community took flesh for the succor of a suffering Mystical Body of Christ, the Church, in prayerful support of her priests.

We firmly believe that Sister Wilhelmina is the most timely and timeless witness to an increasingly self-centered and narrow-minded world. Her beautiful life led to a beautiful death after ninety-five years, seventy-five of which were vowed to God's service and glory. The staggering length of time was a simple composition of daily embraces of God's will at each moment, in a deep spirit of faith and loving perseverance.

Reams have been written in the last half century on the liturgical changes and fallout of the Second Vatican Council, on civil rights, and on the rise in concern for social justice, but few have had the all-encompassing lived experience of our dear Sister Wilhelmina. Her insuperable hope for humanity rested not on her laurels of service, nor in her political views, but in a vision that has been all but forgotten: that her Beloved Spouse, Our Lord Jesus Christ, came not as a secular leader but as a Suffering Servant. His death and resurrection were meant to change our hearts, not our living circumstances. With her unshakeable faith, she never lost sight of the divine mission of her Spouse and of the Church: not to save bodies but to save immortal souls. She understood that suffering, especially in union with Our Lord, was the most effective means to this end. She spoke when necessary, but preached the Gospel far more eloquently in her peaceful and joyful life as a spouse of the Crucified.

We believe she will be reckoned with the great traditional witnesses of the last century, remembered not so much for her persuasive writings, nor her genius, but rather for her very experience as a religious, holding on to the Faith amidst the terrible trials to which the Church has been subject, in resemblance to Christ crucified. From the very trenches, the very heart of the conflict, Sister endured all in union with her Divine Master. Hers was one of the few voices that was willing to point out the mistakes made, allowing water to seep into the bark of Peter. Hers was the fortitude that emerged from the trenches of silence and suffering, and at nearly seventy-five years of age, she reclaimed the Faith lost by almost all around her. She shared the story of a generation of "martyrs" whose suffering is known only to God. She was a true witness to hope in the authentic renewal of religious life for the future, with a clear vision of the Church's supernatural mission, and the self-understanding of nuns as brides of Christ.

Sister Wilhelmina offered her life for the sacred priesthood, which was sadly disfigured in her time, by going back to the very Sacrifice to which it had laid claim for centuries. In the ancient liturgy, she found true union with God that surpassed all human efforts. She truly became one of God's cherished and devoted friends in her love for the unadulterated deposit of faith.

Now on the other side of the veil, Sister Wilhelmina dwells in the very reality to which her life continually pointed, that of the spiritual world. She belongs to the host of witnesses who, like the Divine Bridegroom, are so close to us and always ready to assist us in our own battles. She shows that holiness is possible even in this life, that saints are real, and that miracles do happen. And in her constant battle cry of "God's will!" she attests to the infinite value of each passing moment for storing up treasures in heaven. We were privileged to know her, to dwell with her, and to be called her sisters and intimate friends. We continue to strive to follow her Christlike example, and we earnestly hope that you will come to love her too, and be aided by her powerful assistance from heaven. In the short time that we have been given on this earth, may we all endeavor to imitate Sister Wilhelmina and seek, above all else, "God's will!"

Journeys of Faith and Freedom

*"Although my family was materially poor and I had grown up in
a segregated world, I did not feel myself to be disadvantaged in the
least. Our wealth was our Roman Catholic faith."*

—Sister Wilhelmina

W hen asked to recount her vocation story, Sister Wilhelmina, with her customary love of history, would
begin with the seeds of the Catholic Faith that were sewn in
her family three generations before her birth: "The Faith had
come down to me from my mother's side of the family. One
of my maternal great-grandmothers, Mary Madden, had
been the slave of a French property-holder in St. Genevieve,
Missouri. When Mary became Catholic, her owner freed her
and her young son. 'I cannot keep you in slavery any longer,'
he told her. 'Since you are now baptized, that would be like
keeping Christ in slavery.'"

Mary and her husband, James Alexander Madden, raised

their son, Charles Joseph, in St. Louis, where Mary worked as a cook for a prominent French family named Lucas. Sister Wilhelmina's future grandfather was baptized at the church of St. Elizabeth of Hungary, the Jesuit parish dedicated May 18, 1873, which served the Black Catholics of St. Louis. Charles attended the parish school and served Mass there, at the same church where his granddaughter would also be baptized and attend Mass as a child. His parents, James and Mary, were faithful parishioners of St. Elizabeth's, and they were very close to the parish priest, Fr. Ignatius Panken, SJ. After their deaths in 1883 and 1886, respectively, he not only offered their Requiem Masses, but also buried them in his lot in Calvary Cemetery in St. Louis.

Some years before Charles's birth in 1866, Theodore Grammot LaRose, a free man of African descent who worked as a ship's carpenter, had come from his native island of Santo Domingo to the port of Savannah, Georgia. He decided to settle there, bought some land, and then, as Sister Wilhelmina put it, "set about looking for a bride." He bought a slave woman, Mary Elizabeth, the daughter of an African slave mother and a Cree Indian father; he introduced her to the Catholic Faith and made sure that she was baptized before he married her. It is not certain whether Mary Elizabeth was given this name at her birth or at her baptism, but Sister Wilhelmina was her namesake, for Sister Wilhelmina's mother, Ella Theresa, remembered her half-Indian grandmother fondly: "I knew her well and loved her, the only grandparent that I knew." Theodore LaRose and his wife, Mary Elizabeth, had two children, one of whom was named Mary Louise.

How Mary Louise LaRose of Savannah met and married Charles Joseph Madden of St. Louis is a testimony to Divine Providence; their eldest daughter, Ella Theresa, told the story in a letter written for her grandchildren in the late 1960s. These future grandparents of Sister Wilhelmina both had their own aspirations to dedicate themselves to God's service: Mary Louise had seriously considered becoming an Oblate Sister of Providence, as her granddaughter did in fact become, and Charles pursued a Benedictine vocation, as also his granddaughter would. Ella recounted her father's story:

> When Charles was seventeen years old, his mother died and he began to work at the church [of St. Elizabeth, St. Louis] assisting the sexton and spent most of his time with him in the church basement after work, reading books loaned to him by Father Panken—most of them lives of the saints. He wanted to study for the priesthood and applied to the Benedictine Order. He was refused admission to the monastery but was advised to go to a monastery on an island off the coast of Georgia. This was not a true monastery but a school for Negro boys. He spent two years there as a layman, teaching the youngest boys. Becoming dissatisfied with the conditions at the school, and told that he would not be sent to the regular novitiate house, because he stuttered, he left the island and went to Savannah, Georgia, the nearest city. He was now twenty-one years old. He had five dollars, and a recommendation for work.

He obtained work as an orderly in St. Joseph Catholic Hospital. His intention was to save enough money to return to St. Louis and his family and friends. During this time he met and fell in love with my mother, Mary Louise LaRose, and stayed in Georgia.

Although Charles's original dream of becoming a religious and a priest was not fulfilled, he did become a member of the Third Order of St. Francis and so participated in the religious life as much as he could as a layman. When he passed away in 1936 in St. Louis, he was buried in the brown Franciscan habit, and Franciscan brothers from St. Anthony Church attended his wake and recited the prayers for the dead.

Mary Louise's initial vocational discernment may have been sparked by Mother Mathilda Beasley, Georgia's first Black nun. Mary Louise learned to read and write at a time when educating Black children was illegal in Georgia. Mathilda was most likely Mary Louise's teacher at the secret school she began at their parish. Mathilda later entered the Franciscan Order at York, England, and returned to Savannah two years later to open an orphanage. She settled alongside St. Benedict the Moor parish, founded by Charles's sole remaining former confrere, Father Melchior. Mother Mathilda openly resumed teaching, and supported her own charitable works by sewing.

Perhaps initiated into sewing by Mother Mathilda, Mary Louise pursued this livelihood. As Charles boarded with Mary Louise's sewing instructor, the work occasioned their meeting. Ella related: "My mother, a-seventeen-year-old, was an apprentice seamstress. On a particular night, the dressmaker had a lot of work that had to be gotten [done]. She kept my mother overtime. My father came home while Miss La Rose was still there at the dressmaker's shop. When my mother finished her work, the dressmaker asked Mr. Madden to take her home, and that budded into marriage."

After their marriage, Charles and Mary Louise Madden settled in Tennille, Georgia, where Charles bought land and built a frame-house, which the citizens called "the prettiest house in town." His daughter Ella recorded, "My father disliked being in debt. When the house was finished and he was given the keys, he paid the full cost in cash, $1000."

The Maddens were the only Catholic family in Tennille, so the town had no Catholic church. Ella remembered, "Once a month a priest visited another town, Sandersville, Georgia, three hours away by train, to celebrate Mass and hear confession. My parents made the trip each month to go to confession, hear Mass and receive Communion. . . . Every other summer my mother took us to visit our grandmother [Mary Elizabeth] in Savannah for two weeks. We went to Mass at St. Benedict Catholic Church and the new baby was baptized."

Being the only Catholics in town led to interesting exchanges at Ella's one-room schoolhouse. During recess, the children would chant back and forth on the playground, "Baptist, Baptist is my name, I'm Baptist till I die! I've been baptized in the Baptist church, I'll stay on the Baptist side." "Methodist, Methodist is my name," the other children would chant back in the same fashion. "Mama, are we Baptists or Methodists?" little Ella asked when she got home from school. "You're neither one. You're Catholic." Ella thoughtfully started washing the dishes. Then she remarked, "I know what I'll chant when I get to school: Catholic, Catholic is my name . . ." "Now, don't you go singin' that!" her mother hastily checked her, fearing the backlash from anti-Catholic sentiment.

Charles and Mary Louise supplemented the secular education that their children received, instilling in them a deep love of their Catholic Faith and also a zeal for learning. As Ella recalled, "My father taught me my catechism. My mother taught me my prayers. My father was a student all his life and constantly added books to our home library. He read children's books to me long before I was old enough to attend school. These were happy Sunday afternoons."

When Ella was only ten years old, she lost her beloved grandmother, mother, and baby sister in a single year: Mary Elizabeth died of a stroke, Mary Louise in childbirth, and the baby sister of pneumonia. After a few years, Charles entered a second marriage with Mary Josephine Doley; like Charles and his late wife, Mary Josephine also was a devout Catholic who had pursued a religious vocation. Orphaned at the age of ten, she had been entrusted to St. Katharine Drexel and the Sisters of the Blessed Sacrament at their convent in Cornwells, Pennsylvania. She actually entered the community as a sister but left at the age of twenty; she met and married Charles Madden a few years later in 1905. Mary Josephine's formation under the hand of Mother Drexel and her experience of religious life doubtless contributed to the strong Catholic formation of Sister Wilhelmina's mother.

This second marriage of Charles Madden also makes another connection between Sister Wilhelmina's family history and her life as a religious, both as an Oblate Sister of Providence and as a Benedictine. St. Katharine Drexel had begun her new order, the Sisters of the Blessed Sacrament, at her blood sister's home in Torresdale, Pennsylvania. She called the temporary convent St. Michel. In the meantime, a new convent, St. Elizabeth's, was built two miles down the road from St. Michel, where Mother Drexel received Sister Wilhelmina's step-grandmother. Bishop Ryan of Philadelphia gave Mother Drexel a precious relic of the True Cross that had belonged to St. John Neumann, a friend and part-time chaplain of the Oblate Sisters of Providence. Mother Drexel then encouraged her sister to convert the old convent at St. Michel into a shrine for the relic of the True Cross, which she did. Many years later, the shrine closed, and the pews were sent to the newly founded community of the Benedictines of Mary in 2002. The next year, by God's providence, Sister Wilhelmina happened upon the grounds of St. Michel, so close to the place where her step-grandmother was raised. Without knowing where she was, Sister Wilhelmina found the grave of a priest who would have known Mother Drexel and perhaps also her young charges. Sister was mysteriously moved to recite Psalm 129, "Out of the Depths," the traditional prayer for the dead, with great devotion.

Charles Madden's work transferred him back to St. Louis in 1912, where Ella attended Sumner High School, the oldest and most renowned high school for Black students, with many notable alumni in the fields of music, sports, and education. There, Ella first met her future husband, Oscar Lee Lancaster.

Oscar came from a very different family background. His grandfather, William Lancaster, was an English overseer who had eloped with a slave; their only son, William Jr., strongly resembled his White father and consequently did not suffer any discrimination from the local White society in Tifton, Georgia. As Sister Wilhelmina told the story, however, "William Jr. disappointed his White neighbors when he followed his father's example by marrying black-as-coal Henrietta Green," the daughter of a Baptist minister. They had two sons, the eldest being Oscar Lee Lancaster.

By the age of six, Oscar had lost both his mother and little brother; at the age of twelve, he ran into trouble with his father, the details of which remain unknown. At this point, Oscar had also gotten as far in his education as the little country school for Negroes could take him. Consequently, at the young age of twelve, he ran away from home.

2

Meet Me in St. Louis

Oscar made it to Arkansas and was taken in by a turpentine camp. As his age and strength increased, he was able to support himself by splitting railroad ties. While in his teens, and with only sixteen dollars in his pocket, he came to St. Louis to further his education. There, he attended Sumner High School with Ella Madden. Sister Wilhemina described her parents in their high school years: "Back then, Oscar was a hard-shell Baptist. Ella was a Catholic. He was a star on the football team. She was unimpressed. Indeed, she found him revolting whenever he spoke up in class on account of his atrocious English. So, no, they were *not* high school sweethearts."

After high school, Oscar served in a Black regiment in World War I, serving for two years and eight months overseas in France. Meanwhile, Ella pursued her dream to become a teacher. "All my life," she recalled, "I have had two ambitions, to teach and to write stories." She became reacquainted with Oscar after he returned from the war and introduced him to the Faith. Sister Wilhelmina affirmed that Ella sought to bring Oscar into the Church without the intention of marrying him; on the contrary, Ella had no intention of marrying at all, for in those days the schools in St. Louis did not hire married women as teachers, and she wanted to remain a teacher.

Upon his return to St. Louis, Oscar was hired as business manager for a publishing company, the *St. Louis Tribune.* Oscar approached Ella as a company sales representative, and Ella confessed, "I bought a share just to get rid of him." Nevertheless, Oscar persisted in his Catholic interest and decided to enter the Church in 1921. Ironically, the Antioch Baptist Church to which he belonged was just about to name him minister.

Ella jubilantly brought him to Fr. Joseph P. Lynam, SJ, at the Black parish of St. Elizabeth of Hungary, saying, "This young man wishes to be received into the Church, and I would like to be his godmother." The wise priest looked at her, then looked at him, and stated, "No, you may not be his godmother." He knew that according to the Code of Canon Law at that time, such a relationship would be a spiritual impediment if they would eventually wish to marry.

Ella recounted, "I didn't fall in love with Oscar until after he became Catholic. I realized afterwards, that whenever we talked (when we went to school together) he would ask me questions about the Catholic Church and I answered them." Father Lynam's foresight was salutary; Ella and Oscar were indeed married on July 29, 1922 at St. Elizabeth's with Father Lynam presiding.

Oscar and Ella settled at 4315 Garfield Street in a Black

neighborhood of St. Louis, where he worked long, hard hours as a life insurance salesman. Ella ended her teaching career in order to raise their five children: Oscar Lee Jr., Mary Elizabeth, William Charles (Billy), Christine Marie, and Benjamin Greene.

Mary Elizabeth, who would grow up to become Sister Wilhelmina, was born on Palm Sunday, April 13, 1924, and baptized at the church of St. Elizabeth's, where her parents had been married and where her grandfather, Charles Madden, had been raised.

"I lived with both my parents—along with three brothers and one sister—at 4315 Garfield only seventeen straight years from my birth in Barnes Hospital on April 13, 1924, until my departure for the novitiate of the Oblate Sisters of Providence in September 1941," Sister Wilhelmina remembered. "We shared joys and sorrows, struggles and hardships; we skimped, saved and sacrificed, with my mother carrying the greater portion of the cross."

Despite her lifelong ambitions to teach and to write, Ella subordinated them to her new roles as wife and mother. Sister Wilhelmina gratefully remembered that, despite she and her siblings being "somewhat boisterous," Ella "bravely made the sacrifice of staying at home with us throughout all our growing up years. We could converse with her at any time; she had the patience, humility, and heroic charity to listen to all our childish notions."

Ella's school friends used to visit, Sister Wilhelmina recalled, "to give her advice on how to enjoy life and not be dominated by drab, domestic drudgery." "I remember one visitor very vividly. She was the wife of a high school principal. Laden with perfume and furs she would come with her five-year-old son whom Oscar, Billy and I had to take outside in the backyard with us and entertain. Meanwhile she sat in our plain, sofaless, living room, chatting with her old friend, Ella T., then wearing a plain, gingham house dress and old house shoes. After a while this lady stopped coming; my mother had not been able to return her visits."

The years during the Great Depression were especially difficult for the Lancasters. Sister Wilhelmina recalled one evening at the dinner table when they had no bread. "My brothers and sister and I, we were laughing and playing; we didn't even notice something was missing." Later that night, however, little Mary overheard her mother sobbing, "I have not fed my children today! I have not fed my children today!"

Sister Wilhelmina also described the warm summer day in 1930 when her father came home "crushed with sorrow at the loss of his job as insurance salesman for Liberty Life."

> His world seemed to have come to an end. The insurance company for which he worked had folded. Ella was cooking in the kitchen; and from lines anchored to posts of the back porch there were clothes flapping in the summer breeze. Oscar was sitting in a chair at the kitchen table. He saw his shirt on the line. "I guess that's my last shirt," he said aloud. Ella laughed. She was nearly jovial. "Nonsense!" she cried. "You're not that kind of man." Indeed he wasn't. He went out and got another job with another insurance company— Atlanta Life—the very next day. He went out with the

backing of a woman who believed in him, a woman who had laughed aloud at his fears, and who had gone on with home duty as usual.

Ella Lancaster never consented to take a job herself or to receive welfare money from the government, knowing what a humiliation that would have been to her husband. She preferred to endure their poverty bravely rather than call into question her husband's ability to provide for their family. As her daughter remembered, "Friends would say that it was a shame she couldn't go to work and thus supplement her husband's income. Ella wouldn't hear of such a course of action. Nor would she think of applying for government relief as many of the neighbors were doing. She was determined to live on her husband's income. He wanted to be the provider and she would not crush his manhood."

Oscar used their material hardships as occasions to teach their children responsibility. When Oscar Jr. was six years old and Mary was five, as Sister Wilhelmina remembered, they would sometimes ask their father for a nickel, which he always gave them. But before they could run off with it, Oscar would be called back. "Now, Oscar," his father would say, "How are you going to spend that nickel? I'll give you a nickel every week, but you must learn to budget it. You can't just run off and buy candy with it. You should change it to pennies. You have to save, put some those pennies aside. Look at your shoes; won't you need shoe strings? You have to save to buy yourself new shoe strings!"

Sister Wilhelmina concluded the story, "It was no wonder

that Oscar grew up to become an eminently successful public accountant."

In addition to their struggle with poverty, the Lancaster
family had to endure the hardship of segregation. The Lancasters attended St. Elizabeth's, just as the Maddens had a
generation before; the Negro parish at this time was blessed
with a zealous pastor, Fr. William Markoe, in honor of
whom Sister Wilhelmina would eventually receive her religious name.

3

The Fighting Markoes

Fr. William Markoe and his brother (and fellow-Jesuit priest) Fr. John Markoe, were devoted apostles to the Black population of St. Louis. On the feast of the Assumption of the Blessed Virgin Mary, August 15, 1917, several weeks after the East St. Louis massacre, which left about one hundred Black people dead and hundreds more homeless, Fathers William and John Markoe made the following vow:

> O Jesus, we, the undersigned, resolve and determine, in honor of Thy Sacred Heart, Thy Holy Mother, our Guardian Angels and all our Patron Saints, especially Saint Ignatius and Saint Peter Claver, to give and dedicate our whole lives and all our energies, as far as we are able, and it is not contrary to a pure spirit of pure indifference and obedience, for the work of the salvation of the Negroes in the United States; and though altogether unworthy, we trust in the Sacred Hearts, O Jesus and Mary, to obtain for us the priceless favor of doing so. And do thou, O St. Peter Claver, pray for

us. Amen. Also, daily to repeat this resolution, for the
fulfillment of our expectations and desires.

Born in the 1890s in Minnesota, the Markoe brothers
had virtually no contact with Blacks in their youth, but they
each became devoted to the Black people early on. John,
the elder of the two, entered West Point, where he became
a football star, playing alongside the future President Eisenhower and against Knute Rockne. As a young cadet, John
defended the only Black cadet at the school. He went on
to be assigned to a Black regiment until he was discharged
for a scene of public drunkenness. He consequently entered
the Minnesota National Guard and served honorably in the
Southwest.

Meanwhile, his younger brother William studied for a
year at the university in St. Louis before entering the Jesuit
novitiate in Florissant, just north of St. Louis, in 1913. As a
novice, he frequented the crowded and impoverished Black
communities of downtown St. Louis, bringing them religious instruction as well as material assistance. He wrote
to his brother John, who was then fighting on the Mexican
border, about his work with the Black Catholics of St. Louis,
which seems to have made an impression on his older
brother. Soon, John left the military and himself entered the
Jesuit order at Florissant in 1917.

This was a particularly turbulent time for the Blacks of St.
Louis. The 1916 vote on segregation confined a large section
of the Black population to the Ville, just north of the Cathe-
dral Basilica of St. Louis; the ensuing tension culminated in
the 1917 massacre. This turbulence in the early part of the

twentieth century gave St. Louis a reputation for being a hotbed of interracial strife, which died down in the 1960s, but has resurfaced in more recent times. In response to this violence, the Markoe brothers made their vow and dedicated the rest of their lives to the service of the Black people.

William furthered his studies in Spokane, where he continued his Black ministry and authored a book on St. Peter Claver, *The Slave of the Negroes.* Returning to St. Louis in 1923, before he was even ordained a priest, he made two hundred Black converts in nine months, largely by walking through Black neighborhoods, calling on families, and bringing food and supplies. That same year, he wrote to Mother Katharine Drexel, begging her to send sisters to St. Louis. She consented, sending Blessed Sacrament Sisters the next year to aid him at St. Nicholas parish where he catechized many souls.

Father William was ordained at St. Francis Xavier Church at St. Louis University in 1926; many Black people attended, despite of the initial refusal of Father William's superiors. The following year, he was made pastor of St. Elizabeth's, where both Markoe brothers were eventually assigned. Father William served as pastor there until 1941, with only a brief interval away in service to Negro organizations. He devoted a tireless amount of energy to the parish. After a tornado severely damaged the old church building in the late 1920s, Father William acquired a former mansion on Pine Street to use as a church building. The parish's new location, about an hour's walk from the Lancasters' home, was outside the Black sector of St. Louis, and so some opponents to the construction of a Black church within a White sector scheduled a protest meeting. Father William recalled in his autobiography: "We held a council of war. My brother being a West Pointer and an old army man was a good strategist. He had also played football on the same squad with Ike Eisenhower. We decided we should cover the un-Catholic anti-Negro meeting."[1]

Father John and another friend attended the protest meeting in civilian dress in order to remain incognito, taking down and then publishing the speeches, which criticized not only Fr. William Markoe but also the archbishop of St. Louis, who had given his approval to the parish's relocation. As a result, the leaders of the opposition were shamed into silence, and the parish move continued unimpeded.

The new parish also lay within the boundaries of Visitation Parish, which would host the St. Joseph Reunion for the alumni of the Catholic High School for Negroes, which Ella and Oscar Lancaster would help to found. The pastor of Visitation Parish was Msgr. Cornelius Flavin, the brother of Bishop Glennon Flavin of Lincoln and the pastor of the future Cardinal Dolan. In addition to sponsoring the St. Joseph Reunion, he was a vigorous champion of racial integration.

Father William began *The St. Elizabeth's Chronicle*, which eventually became the *Interracial Review*, taken over by Fr. John LaFarge. Father LaFarge was son of the artist who pioneered the stained-glass style eventually attributed to Louis Comfort Tiffany. Father LaFarge, future editor of

---

[1]   As quoted in Cyprian Davis, *The History of Black Catholics in the United States*, 224.

America magazine, was originally a great ally of the Markoes, but they eventually distanced themselves since they felt he was too condescending in his approach to ministry among the Black population.

Another ally was the great writer and playwright Fr. Daniel Lord, SJ, who frequented St. Elizabeth's Parish and made a point of including its parishioners in his productions. In her later years, Sister Wilhelmina still lit up whenever anyone sang Father Lord's hymn to Christ the King, and she would join in with gusto. An unknown but tantalizing question is whether Sister Wilhelmina ever crossed paths with the future Mother Mary Francis, PCC. Mother Mary Francis, abbess of the Poor Clare Monastery in Roswell, New Mexico, and brave defender of traditional religious life during the 1970s and 1980s, was herself a native of St. Louis, three years older than Sister Wilhelmina, and also closely associated with Fr. Daniel Lord at the same time.

A later and powerful friend was Fr. Claude Heithaus, SJ, whose explosive sermon at St. Francis Xavier College Church in 1944 attacked the continuing practice of rejecting Black applicants to college, even as one of Sister Wilhemina's classmates had been rejected on account of her race. Sister Wilhelmina's own sister Christine benefited from Father Heithaus's efforts. She was one of the first Black women admitted to the University of Saint Louis in the years that followed, even being offered a scholarship.

Apart from these rare exceptions, the Markoes were not supported by the hierarchy nor by their fellow priests. In 1941, Father William was reassigned to Mankato, Minnesota, where he lamented that "not a single Negro lived."

Sister Wilhelmina was therefore the last young woman whom Fr. William Markoe directed to the religious life before his northern exile, following St. Elizabeth Parishioners Sister Claude, Sister Philomena, Sister Incarnata, and Sister Eulalia. Father William briefly took up his work later in his assignment in Denver but was then assigned to teach theology at Marquette, again limiting his apostolate. He supported his brother's work in Omaha from a distance until his death in Milwaukee in 1969.

4

My Heart Is Set

Growing up in a poor Black neighborhood amid all the turbulence of interracial strife, Mary Lancaster nevertheless did not become a bitter victim of discrimination. Much later, as an elderly nun, she composed a couplet that no doubt echoed her own childhood: "A child's business is to play; without it he has lost the day." As a little girl, she and her playmates had to pass through a White neighborhood to get to the library. "And we were runnin'!" she vividly recalled, lest they, as Black children, should get into trouble in a White neighborhood. A little White boy sitting on his front porch called to her, "Hiya, chocolate drop!" Without skipping a beat, she called back, "Hello, marshmallow!" When asked how the remarked was received, Sister said, "I don't know, we just kept on runnin'!" Another asked if the White boy spoke unkindly. Sister punned, "Oh no, he was a sweet boy!"

No doubt she inherited this buoyant spirit and strength of soul from her parents. As an elderly sister, Sister Wilhelmina copied the oft-quoted poem by Edward Tuck, to which she added the title "Ella Theresa Madden Lancaster's Philosophy":

> Age is a quality of mind.
> If you have left your dreams behind,
> If hope is cold,
> If you no longer look ahead,
> If your ambitions' fires are dead,
> Then you are old.

> But if from life you take the best,
> And if in life you keep the jest,
> If love you hold,
> No matter how the years go by,
> No matter how the birthdays fly,
> You are not old.

Despite segregation and material hardships, the Lancasters found their wealth and their dignity in their Faith. While her children attended catechism classes at St. Elizabeth's on Sunday, Ella Lancaster attended an informal course on theology for the laity taught by Fr. William Markoe. She later wrote, "It was joy for me. When the opportunity came to help neighbors who came to me for counsel I was able to help. Many came to learn about the Catholic religion, or rather to discuss what they thought about White Catholics—prejudice, bigotry, Negro pride, etc. In time many decided they wanted instruction in Catholic Christian doctrine but did not want to go to a priest. Father Markoe gave me permission and I became an authorized catechist."

In an essay entitled "The Negro Looks at Catholicism," published in *The Interracial Review*, Ella wrote that many Black people considered the Catholic Church in America as the White man's church. She observed that the real obstacle to conversion was not doctrine but prejudice: "Those who have studied with me have had no difficulty in accepting the Catholic Church as the one true Church established by Christ for the salvation of men. Acts of prejudice perpetrated against them by White Catholics have been the obstacle that made it difficult for them to enter the Church. If all Catholics in America, White and Negro, kept the two great commandments of love of God and love of neighbor, I believe we would see in America in our day mass conversion of the Negro to Catholicism."

Ella Lancaster practiced what she preached. "My father was the first convert that my mother helped to make," Sister Wilhelmina recounted. "Before her death in 1986, she had helped to make at least a hundred more."

Little Mary was particularly affected by her mother's zeal and also by a tender love for the Blessed Virgin Mary. One of her earliest memories was a vision of Our Lady: when Mary Lancaster was only two years old and sitting in her high chair, she saw the Blessed Virgin Mary appear to her and smile at her. The rest of her family remembered this event and handed down the story, as one of Sister Wilhelmina's nieces recalled more than ninety years later.

Sister Wilhelmina's most beloved way of honoring the Blessed Mother was the recitation of the Most Holy Rosary. Even as a seven-year-old child, Mary asked her siblings and playmates to pray the Rosary with her. When they refused, she tearfully had recourse to her mother, who replied that she should pray it by herself, which she did. This was the occasion of her second encounter with the Blessed Mother, who appeared to her and thanked her.

On another occasion, Oscar and Billy had gone off to the river to fish while their sister was at home playing in the yard. Suddenly, Mary bolted into the house, exclaiming, "Mama, we've got to pray the Rosary right now!" Her mother hesitated, surprised at her daughter's outburst, but Mary insisted that they must pray immediately for her brothers Oscar and Billy. So Ella consented and prayed the Rosary with her little daughter. When the boys returned, their mother asked them about their fishing excursion. At first, they replied that it had been fine, but when she persisted in her questioning, they confessed that the boat had capsized, and they had been afraid that they would drown. They were not sure why or how, but they managed to get back to the shore safely.

"Did it happen at such-and-such a time?" Ella queried, citing the time when Mary had rushed into the house. Yes, it was at that time," the boys answered. "Well, your sister was praying for you, that's why," Ella replied.

Sister Wilhelmina remained a faithful and zealous proponent of the Holy Rosary all her life, even adding it to her religious name when she took vows as a Benedictine of Mary, becoming Sister Mary Wilhelmina of the Most Holy Rosary.

Ella continued bringing up her children with a deep spirit of piety. One prayer Sister Wilhelmina particularly remembered her teaching the youngsters was:

Jesus, Mary and Joseph I give you my heart
 and my soul;
Jesus, Mary, and Joseph, assist me in my last
 agony.
Jesus, Mary and Joseph may I breathe forth
 my spirit in peace with you. Amen.

After repeating the prayer with them, Oscar suddenly looked up and said "Mama, is Benjamin gonna die?" Ella then explained that the prayer was to help them when they would die.

This is the day when you begin to really live!
The day when Jesus, whole, entire, to you
 does give
Himself: His Risen Body with His Precious
 Blood
To strengthen you for life eternal as your
 food!
You've just existed; you have never lived
 before
This glorious day; but now you'll live
 forevermore!

Being raised strong in the Faith, little Mary was well prepared for the grace of a religious vocation. This call came very early, with her first reception of Holy Communion, and her response was immediate and irrevocable. In her own words:

I had scarlet fever when I was eight, so I couldn't make
 my first Communion till I was nine. I received my

vocation on my First Communion day. On April 2, 1934, I made my first Holy Communion, an unforgettable experience, when Our Lord asked me, "Will you be mine?" He seemed to be such a handsome and wonderful man, I agreed immediately. Then He told me to meet Him every Sunday at Holy Communion: "You come to Communion every time you come to Mass," He said. I said nothing about this conversation to anyone, believing that everyone that went to Holy Communion heard Our Lord talk to them."

Sister Wilhelmina continued the story of her first Holy Communion: "Well, the next week, I got up and got a drink of water like I usually did. Back then, water broke the fast required for Holy Communion. I went crying to my mother, 'Mama, I broke my fast, I can't receive Communion.' 'Now you stop that foolishness,' Mama replied, 'You can receive Communion next week.'"

This commonsense reply did not console Mary, and as she remained in her pew while everyone else went up to receive Communion, she could not check her tears. This was more than her father could bear, so he ran after the priest to ask for a dispensation for his little daughter. Whether he obtained this dispensation is not recorded, but Sister Wilhelmina never forgot the tender solicitude of her father in this attempt. "That same, unfortunate, drink-water Sunday, April 9," Sister Wilhelmina concluded her memories of that day, "I was confirmed."

Mary remained faithful to her weekly meetings with Our Lord at Holy Communion, but as she later confessed,

"In those days I hardly knew what belonging to Our Lord meant." The seed of a religious vocation lay hidden for several years.

Mary's faith helped her face the opposition both of segregation on the one hand and anti-Catholic sentiment on the other. She wrote:

> The public school that I attended—John Marshall Elementary—was only two blocks away from my house. Also two blocks away, in another direction, was Holy Ghost Catholic Church. Although long ago demolished, that church and its atmosphere are still vivid in my memory. What a difference a few steps from the sidewalk made! Once across the threshold, I was awestruck by that quiet place where sunlight streamed through multi-colored glass windows and played upon dark oaken pew and marble columns. The church had been built by Germans years before. The neighborhood had once been their neighborhood. In my childhood the congregation was still for the most part German: they returned in their cars every Sunday to worship there. My family and a few others like us sat in the rear of the church on the left side. The people in this section were the last ones to approach the Communion rail, but when I knelt to receive the Lord I felt no loss or deprivation whatever. My mother had taught me from my infancy that the church was God's house, and that the Lord Jesus Christ was truly present in the most holy Sacrament of the Altar. "What does it matter," she would say when talk of discrimination

against us arose, "whether you are first or last in line, you receive the Lord!"

I was taunted at times by my schoolmates for my adherence to Catholicism. Words of ridicule and dis-approval still resound: "You fool! You are going to the white man's church!" I would stand up to them with the emphatic reply, "I belong to the Church that Christ established for all people!" Of course the chil-dren would laugh at me. . . .

At last, several years later, my confessor, Father Lawrence Rost, whom I saw every Saturday at Holy Ghost Church two blocks up the street, asked if I ever thought about being a Sister. I had not of course, but he thought I could be a good Sister. I went to work on the idea right away and wrote to the superior of the Oblate Sisters of Providence in Baltimore, Maryland for direction.

This letter, preserved by the Oblate Sisters of Providence, displays Mary's single-heartedness and forthrightness, which remained two of her most signal characteristics; it is also written in her flawless penmanship, which she maintained to the end of her life:

4315 Garfield
St. Louis, Missouri
May 6, 1937

Dear Mother Superior,

I am a girl, thirteen years old, and I would like to become a nun. I plan to come to your convent as soon

as possible. I will graduate from Grade School next
month. What I want to know is, whether you have to
bring anything to the convent and what it is that you
have to bring. I hope I am not troubling you any, but
I have my heart set on becoming a nun. (Of course I
am a Catholic.)

God bless you and those under your command.

Respectfully,
Mary Elizabeth Lancaster

Sister Wilhelmina recalled the superior's response:
"Mother Mary Consuella Clifford wrote me back, told me
that I was too young to enter the convent and advised that I
finish high school first. She advised that I go to the Blessed
Sacrament Sisters' school in Rock Castle, Virginia. The odd
part about this advice is that the Oblate Sisters of Providence had a school for girls right there in St. Louis: St. Rita's
Academy."

So Mary Lancaster's pursuit of her vocation was temporarily delayed until her secondary education was completed,
but the few Catholic options necessitated a new school.

5

Ite Ad Joseph

A round the time of Mary's graduation from Marshall and her letter to Mother Consuella, Ella and Oscar were enlisted in an enterprise. The Sisters of St. Joseph of Carondelet staffed St. Matthew's School in the Ville. One of them, Sister Anna Joseph Bercherer, saw the urgent need for continuity in a Black Catholic high school. This urgency increased after the Christian Brothers' McBride High School denied the entrance of a group of Black boys in 1937. Obtaining the support and permission of her superior, Mother Tarcisia, Sister Anna Joseph approached the Lancasters to help establish a Black Catholic high school in that same year, 1937. Though Marshall was a public school, Sister Wilhelmina recalled, "My parents, who did not want me to go to the public high school, got to work and founded St. Joseph's Catholic High School for Negroes which lasted until Archbishop Ritter put an end to segregation of Negroes in the Diocese." All five of the Lancaster children graduated from this school that their parents founded.

Others generously contributed their help and expertise, such as Redemptorist Fr. Donald Corrigan, who simultaneously taught Latin and math at St. Joseph College and Seminary. St. Louis seminarian Patrick Molloy led a formidable athletics department, which played its way into integration by challenging local White schools; it went on to become the first Negro team to belong to the State High School Athletic Association. Father Molloy continued his work at St. Joseph's after his ordination. Mary began her studies at St. Joseph's High School in its inaugural year.

> During my four years in high school I sort of put the idea of becoming a Sister on the back burner and applied myself to learning as much as I could about everything there was to learn. Unfortunately, my parents spoiled me and let me sit down much too much to books and papers when I should have been up cooking, sewing and doing household work. My mother was a bookworm, too, and she is mentioned in the little book, *Negro Catholic Writers*, which mentions her as being deceased many years before her death actually happened. Underground or along with the religious desire was my desire to become a writer. I wrote my first poem, or rhyme, when I was in the 4th grade and was made over for it as someone special. I soon had a notebook full of rhymes, but this was not what I really wanted. I wanted to write stories, good fiction, like *Little Women*, and so on.

Mary never lost her love of words; she continued to write verses throughout her religious life, filling dozens of notebooks to succeed this first one written during her childhood years.

By the time she graduated as valedictorian in 1941, the school had gained state accreditation. It was the first accredited Black Catholic high school in Missouri, making Mary Elizabeth Lancaster the first recognized graduate. Her diploma was signed by the diocesan superintendent Charles Helmsing, the future bishop of Kansas City-St. Joseph, the diocese wherein Mary Lancaster, as a Benedictine of Mary, would finish her life.

The struggle for integration continued on the college level. One of Mary Lancaster's classmates, Mary Aloyse Foster, was denied admission to Webster College in Webster Groves, Missouri, following their graduation. Fr. John Markoe used this refusal as ammunition to break down the racial barrier in St. Louis colleges, where even Catholic colleges such as Webster denied the admission of Blacks. Ironically, Sister Wilhelmina studied music at Webster College from 1953 till 1955, twelve years after Mary Aloyse was refused. Ethel Mattie Williams, another schoolmate of Mary Lancaster, finally succeeded in being among the first five Blacks admitted to St. Louis University in 1944. This motivated Archbishop Ritter to begin integration of schools in his diocese, threatening excommunication for resistance. He ordered all Catholics to attend the parish closest to them, which effectively shut down St. Elizabeth's Parish for Blacks only. The parish closed in 1949.

Two Oblate Sisters of Providence attended Mary's graduation on June 1, 1941. One of them was twenty-two-year-old Sister Philomena Micheau, who was currently stationed at the Oblates' school in St. Louis and whose brother was a member of Mary Lancaster's graduating class. Sister Wilhelmina recalled their meeting, which manifests again her customary forthrightness: "The day of my graduation from high school, two Oblate Sisters of Providence were present. When I walked out of the church, I went straight to them standing in the vestibule and told them that I wanted to be one of them. They were shocked, and I was satisfied that I had done what had to be done."

At the time, there were only two religious orders for Black or Hispanic women in the United States. Sister Wilhelmina's pastor, Fr. William Markoe, guided her to one, the Oblate Sisters of Providence. Mother Mary Elizabeth Lange, a Haitian refugee, founded this active community of Black sisters in the early nineteenth century, primarily for the Christian education of colored children.

Mother Lange was born Elizabeth Clarisse Lange in a Haitian community in Santiago de Cuba around 1784 and received an excellent education. Strife following the slave uprising in Haiti in the late 1700s led to her departure from Cuba to the United States. The oral tradition of the Oblates of Providence relates that she arrived first in Charleston, South Carolina, then traveled to Norfolk, Virginia, and finally settled in Baltimore, Maryland, in 1813.

Baltimore's free Black population already outnumbered the slave population, and there was also a sizeable French-speaking African Caribbean population that had fled the Haitian revolt. Baltimore had few educational opportunities for Black children, especially for the poor. There were no free public schools for Black children in Baltimore until

1866. The few Protestant schools for Black students could not meet the demands of Baltimore's growing free Black population, especially the Catholics. Elizabeth Lange recognized the urgent need, and opened a free school in her home in the Fells Point area of the city with the help of another Carribean woman.

Elizabeth Lange met a Sulpician priest at Baltimore in 1828: Fr. James Marie Hector Joubert dela Muraille, a native Frenchman and former soldier. He had also fled the Haitian slave revolt and headed off teaching catechism to the young refugees who attended Mass at the Lower Chapel at Saint Mary's Seminary. Their illiteracy made for slow progress, so Father Joubert asked Elizabeth to consider founding an order of Sisters to teach and care for Black children. With the addition of two more women, a community began to form, and gained diocesan approval in 1829.

In a document composed for the 160th anniversary of the Oblates' foundation in 1989, entitled "A Sesquicentennial Salute," Sister Wilhelmina takes up the story of these humble origins of her community:

> Just as Americans in this late Twentieth Century are divided over the question of whether or not a child in his mother's womb is a human being with a right to life, so in the early Nineteenth Century people were divided over the question of whether or not the slaves had souls. It was in this milieu that the Oblate Sisters of Providence were founded, as a religious institute, July 2, 1829.

Their original oblation was a promise of obedience to the Archbishop of Baltimore, at that time the Most Reverend James Whitfield, and to their superior chosen from among themselves, she then being Sister Mary, the former Elizabeth Lange.

Three years later, on July 2, 1832, the Sisters made vows of poverty, chastity and obedience. The original four had by that time been joined by five others. . . .

A significant step in between these two events—these two wonderful July seconds—was the community's entry into the association of Holy Slavery of Mary the Mother of God, or, their formal inauguration of the practice of the True Devotion taught by St. Louis Marie Grignon de Montfort. (He was Venerable then.) It happened on July 2, 1830: the entrants were altogether nine persons, including the founder, Reverend James Marie Hector Nicholas Joubert de la Muraille. July second, throughout the years, has been regarded by the Oblate Sisters of Providence as their day of triple consecration, the fountainhead of all their spirituality which has ensued.

As the founding superior of the new community, Mother Mary Lange entrusted the community to the patronage of St. Frances of Rome, a widow and Benedictine oblate. Sister Wilhelmina adds a note about St. Frances of Rome in the same essay:

Francesca, daughter of Paul and Jacobella Bussa, was born in Rome in the year 1384. Her mother was a very devout person, in the habit of visiting every day some of the churches. Francesca, from her infancy, was a pious child. She wanted to give herself completely to God as a religious, but her father refused to go along with this desire and ordered her, when she was twelve years old, to marry the wealthy nobleman, Lorenzo Ponziano. Guided by her confessor, Don Antonio Savello, Francesca made the sacrifice of her own will to God's will and married Lorenzo, to whom she bore six children.

While Francesca was a married woman seeing to the education of her children and working in behalf of her sick, poor neighbors, God assigned an archangel to her as a visible guardian. She saw him always for the remainder of her life, which was long and full of trials. Francesca never gave up assiduous prayer.

Four of her six children having died as infants and her husband's health having begun to decline, Francesca began laying the foundation of the Oblates of Mary of Mount Olivet of the Benedictine Order. Other women, under Francesca's encouragement and guidance, gave themselves to fasting, to prayer and to charitable services. Consecrating themselves to the Blessed Virgin Mary on the feast of the Assumption in the year 1425, they eventually became the original members of this group. Not until after the death of her husband several years later was Francesca able to join the community which she herself had founded. Today she is hailed as a model for young girls, the example of

a devout matron, and finally a true widow, according
to the very pattern drawn up by St. Paul.

Perhaps Mother Mary Lange's choice of this patroness
was St. Frances's devotion to the education of her children and to corporal and spiritual works of mercy for the
poor. The very Rule of the Oblate Sisters of Providence had
many Benedictine practices and overtones, and also a special consecration to the Blessed Virgin, as did St. Frances's
community of oblates. This Benedictine and Marian influence formed Mother Mary's spiritual daughter, Sister Wilhelmina, who in God's providence would one day become a
foundress herself of a new community of oblates, the future
Benedictines of Mary.

With just the four founding sisters and twenty students,
Mother Mary Lange opened a Catholic school for girls in
a rented house at 5 St. Mary's Court in Baltimore. Thus
began St. Frances Academy, the oldest continuously operat-
ing school for Black Catholic children in the United States;
the academy continues to educate children in Baltimore to
this day.

Enduring untold hardships, the oblate sisters sought to
evangelize the Black community through Catholic education. In addition to schools, the sisters later conducted night
classes for women, vocational and career training, and established homes for widows and orphans.

They also gave themselves generously to other acts of
charity. A cholera epidemic broke out in Baltimore in 1832,
when the community numbered just eleven members. The
city officials had asked the Sisters of Charity for eight

sisters to serve the victims of the epidemic, but had only
received four, so they sought help from Father Joubert, who
approached the little community of the Oblates of Providence. The Sisters of Charity were, by the spirit of their
institute, obliged to look after the sick, he told the sisters,
whereas the Oblates of Providence were dedicated to the
education of Black children, but he hoped that the oblates
"would not have less charity than the daughters of St. Paul."
When he then asked for volunteers to risk their lives in nurs-
ing the cholera victims, the entire community rose. He only
chose four, however: Mother Mary Lange herself and three
companions. So great was the danger of death that the only
sister who had not yet made religious profession was allowed
to do so at the morning Mass the next day before setting
out to minister to the sick and dying. Father Joubert later
recalled his sermon to the sisters at that Mass: "I addressed
a few words to them on the good work they were about to
undertake, on the merits attached to the sacrifice they were
making to God of the life He had given them. I pointed out
to them the dangers to which they were obliged to expose
themselves in thus devoting themselves to the service of the
sick poor. . . . I told them that if God permitted that they
should be victims of their zeal, they would die martyrs of
charity."[2] One of these heroic Oblates of Providence did
indeed obtain such a martyrdom of charity.

The death of Father Joubert in 1843 was a crisis for the
oblates, who no longer had a chaplain to offer daily Mass

---

[2]   As quoted in Cyprian Davis, *The History of Black Catholics in
the United States*, 101–2.

for them and to support them in their struggle to maintain their fledging community. Not many were supportive of the small convent of Black sisters. Yet Divine Providence intervened: the sisters' convent adjoined a Redemptorist parish, in the care of St. John Neumann, who not only served the sisters' spiritual needs, but also introduced them to another Redemptorist priest named Fr. Thaddeus Anwander. So great was Father Anwander's concern for the oblates that, on his knees, he begged St. John Neumann, his superior, to serve as the oblates' chaplain. He proved to be a second father and founder of the oblates.

From the community's inception in 1829 until her death on February 3, 1882, Mother Mary Lange never ceased to spend herself for the community. For some years, she even worked as a domestic servant at St. Mary's Seminary in Baltimore to help support her sisters. The community's diary records the delicate balance that the Black sisters strove to maintain as religious while undertaking such menial work: "We do not conceal the difficulty of our situation as persons of color and religious at the same time, and we wish to conciliate these two qualities in such a manner as not to appear too arrogant on the one hand and on the other, not to miss the respect which is due to the state we have embraced and the holy habit which we have the honor to wear."[3]

Sister Wilhelmina inherited from her spiritual mother this humble self-effacement united to a deep understanding of

---

[3] As quoted in Cyprian Davis, *The History of Black Catholics in the United States*, 102.

the dignity of her religious state, particularly as manifested in the holy habit.

The difficult beginning of the oblate sisters, with challenges from poverty, racial discrimination, and periods without a chaplain, was not without consolations and even times of lightheartedness. Sister Wilhelmina gladly shared one of these stories, preserved through the oblates' oral tradition: at a profession ceremony in the very early days of the community, when the oblates' chapel was located on a busy inner-city street of Baltimore, the chaplain, possibly Father Joubert himself, solemnly asked the sisters about to make profession, "Beloved daughters, what do you wish?" But before they could respond with the formal request to profess vows, the raucous call of a street vendor blared through the open chapel window for all to hear: "Hot devilled crabs!" The community and congregation burst into laughter, and Sister Wilhelmina herself could never retell this story without a chuckle.

6

See That Door?

Mary Lancaster did not hesitate to follow through on her decision to become an Oblate Sister of Providence; she departed for the oblates' novitiate house in Baltimore just a few months after her graduation. Her parents, Oscar and Ella, grieved to say goodbye to their beloved eldest daughter; in her old age, Sister Wilhelmina still remembered her mother's tears at their parting. The two were very like-minded in their love of learning and particularly of writing, but they were especially close through their mutual devotion to their Catholic Faith. This Faith, however, strengthened them to make the sacrifice of parting, and Mary boarded the train to follow the Lord wherever He would lead her. Sister Wilhelmina recalled, "So that September, at age 17, I left my parents' house for Baltimore, Maryland. Sister Philomena Micheau, one of the Sisters who attended my graduation and who was superior of St. Frances Home for Girls in Normandy, gave me a trunk. Two of her Sisters who happened to be going to Baltimore accompanied me on my journey there in September."

Mary had no illusions about the challenges of the novitiate. She recalled in later years, "I knew that the novitiate was a time of trial during which the community would look me over and decide whether I had a vocation to it or not." When she and her band of classmates arrived at the oblates' novitiate house in Baltimore, they were greeted by the novice mistress, Sister Mary Inez Calthirst. "See that door?" Sister Inez turned to the newly arrived group of postulants and pointed with a foreboding air to the door through which they had just entered to commence their novitiate. "It swings both ways!"

Sister Philomena, who had seen Mary to the station in St. Louis, became novice mistress of the community just after Sister Wilhelmina's profession. Sister Wilhelmina probably would have preferred to have been formed by her, having already known her as a fellow St. Louisan, but accepted God's providence in her formation under Sister Inez. She nevertheless carried Sister Philomena's promise of prayer with her for the remainder of her life. A visible reminder of this was the cross Sister Philomena gave Sister Wilhelmina, which was affixed to her rosary. Sister Wilhelmina cherished the gift and used the rosary until she misplaced it in 2001.

Sister Inez, on the other hand, had deep psychological problems, which were made especially manifest the year after Sister Wilhelmina's profession and after the novitiate building burned down. Some of Sister Wilhelmina's stories about her novitiate days hinted at Sister Inez' strict discipline, but Sister Wilhelmina never made a complaint about her. Rather, she seemed grateful for the sense of sacrifice that Sister Inez instilled in her novices.

Sister Wilhelmina's faith in the Lord's personal love for her sustained her from the very first day of her novitiate. Years later, she recalled: "That September day, when I entered the novitiate chapel for the first time, that same Lord Who spoke to me in my First Communion, welcomed me lovingly, put His arms around me and promised that from then on I would be His."

In March 1942, after the initial period of postulancy, Mary Lancaster exchanged a white bridal gown for her religious habit, which she treasured until the day of her death as the sign of her consecration as a bride of Christ. All the postulants were allowed to submit several suggestions for their religious name; Mary Lancaster's great devotion to St. John the Baptist prompted her to write "Sr. Mary Baptista." But her formators advised her, "No, you should ask for 'Wilhelmina,' since you are the last sister sent by Fr. William Markoe." So Mary added, "Sr. Mary Wilhelmina," as a second choice. This was the name she received, much to her disappointment, as she later admitted. Here again, however, Divine Providence entrusted her to the patronage of a great Benedictine, St. William the Abbot.

As a novice, Sister Mary Wilhelmina eagerly studied the Rule and history of her community. She developed a deep and trusting abandonment to Divine Providence. As an old nun, she would walk the halls of the convent, beating time with her cane and chanting her "Marching Song":

> God's will, God's will, God's will be done!
> Praise we the Father! Praise we the Son!
> Praise we Divine Love, Lord Holy Ghost!
> Praise we in union with the heavenly host!

The notes that she made in her personal copy of the 1986 edition of the oblates' constitutions further indicate the zeal she had for the original spirit of her order. In this passage, she underlines the key words:

> Our dependence on Divine Providence is closely woven in the fabric of our history. The way we understand our <u>charism</u> and live out the religious ideals of our founders is one of <u>union with God</u> through His providential care of us. It was this <u>charism</u> which sustained our foundress in those early days of trial and frustration. Our motto, *Providentia Providebit*, is the legacy she handed down to us and which sustains us in our service of humanity. This Providence spirituality impels the Oblate Sister of Providence to serve others in love and prepares her to enter even more deeply into God. Her ever-deepening <u>union with God</u> enables her to perform the highest service, handing over to others what she has received in prayer.[4]

These words, "charism" and "union with God," profoundly resonated with her who had embraced religious life as a life of fidelity to the Lord with whom she was so deeply in love.

---

[4]   *Response to Love: Constitutions and Directives of the Oblate Sisters of Providence*, 5.

In the margins of this copy of the constitutions, she adds in her own hand, "Our <u>first</u> constitution, drawn up by Fathers Joubert and Tessier, stated: 'The Sisters shall form but one class, and all shall wish with joy to do the meanest work.'" Throughout her religious life, Sister Wilhelmina never shirked any task given her, no matter how tedious or unpleasant. As a novice, she had no teaching engagements, but much training in domestic chores. "We did a lot of SWIC," she remembered, "Sweeping, Washing, Ironing and Cooking." "Get wood," was the command she most frequently received. So off she would go, no matter the weather, to chop and split wood all day.

She kept her high spirits at all times, even after her newly earned driver's license was taken away. "It felt so *good* to be out driving!" she recalled. "The problem was that I turned right when I *saw* the intersection . . . right into a man's parked car." Years later, when a novice took Sister Wilhelmina, then in her eighties, for a car ride, the novice asked her if she would like to take the wheel. Sister Wilhelmina replied, "Not unless you want to go up one side of the tree and down the other!"

She often recalled another novitiate misadventure: "I got new high-top boots. I was so proud of them until I fell down the stairs with a whole stack of plates." If a sister broke anything, her penance would be to kneel in the refectory holding the broken item before being permitted to eat, so Sister Wilhelmina's fellow novices cried out, "Oh, Sister Wilhelmina, how're you gonna hold all those?" As her novice mistress inspected Sister Wilhelmina's wrist, lacerated by the broken dishes, Sister Wilhelmina quoted their monthly meditation on the Passion: "And the red blood ran down!" To which Sister Inez retorted, "When you get better, I'm gonna punish you!" Returning to her companions, Sister Wilhelmina continued quoting the meditation, "I have trodden the wine press alone." Finishing the story years later, she would add confidentially, "And I never did get better!"

On another occasion, some newspapers were accidentally delivered to the novitiate; the young sisters in formation had limited contact with the outside world, especially through secular media, and so decided to take advantage of this rare occurrence. The group of them immediately found and divided the comic strips, which they were enjoying when Sister Inez unexpectedly appeared. Sister Wilhelmina imitated her terse assessment of the situation: "I don't think you're gonna find those funnies as funny as you think you are!"

Although Sister Wilhelmina did not return to St. Louis until years later as a professed sister, she maintained her precious family ties. One of her joys as a novice, she recalled, was a letter about her father, who, sharing his wife's missionary zeal, brought his own father into the Catholic Church: "I learned that my father had gone back to Georgia to help his own father, William Lancaster Jr., on his deathbed. My grandfather had lived his life without any religious faith to speak of, interested only in raising hogs and corn and making regular visits to the saloon in town. My father found the nearest Catholic priest and brought him to the bedridden old man. With my father's encouragement, Grandfather Lancaster received instruction in the Catholic faith and was baptized by the priest. He died peacefully the next day."

Sister Wilhelmina's time of formation included growth in her devotion to the Blessed Mother:

> My two and a half years in the novitiate were a happy time, during which I learned from a fellow novice, thirteen years older than I was, about True Devotion to Mary taught by St. Louis De Montfort. We had no book about it; Sr. Alma simply reiterated emphatically that I had no true devotion to Mary because I did not belong to her as her slave. I was so moved by this that I went to the novice-mistress, Sr. Mary Inez Calthirst, and asked if I could become a slave of Mary, like Sr. Alma was. Sr. Inez, amused, grabbed the chain I was wearing and said that this was the sign that all Oblates were slaves of Mary. The miraculous medal and chain were placed around the neck of each novice when she received the habit.

Sister Wilhelmina wore her beloved miraculous medal through her entire religious life, including her last years as a Benedictine of Mary; her new order continued the tradition of placing the blessed medal and chain around the neck of each young woman being received into the community. As an elderly sister, Sister Wilhelmina would devoutly kiss the medal whenever she put it on in the morning or took it off at night and would pray the inscription aloud, "O Mary, conceived without sin, pray for us who have recourse to thee!" She never failed to add her own intentions: "And for those who do NOT have recourse to thee, especially freemasons, atheists, abortionists . . ." In her late eighties and early nineties, she always concluded with, "Obama and his wife and daughters!" And in the very last years of her life, "Donald Trump and his family!"

Sister Wilhelmina also brought her love of writing with her into religious life and dedicated it to the service of her Beloved Lord and His Blessed Mother. Her earliest extent poem dates from this time, around 1944:

Saturday Prayer

Sweet Lady, thanks for all your care for us!
You've been so good—we have no right to
    fuss.
Yet we entreat thee not to think us grown
And reach out all on our own.
We are thy babes, in diapers, not in silk;
We're but newborn and howling for thy milk;
Nay! We are in thy womb, frail seed, unborn:
Oh, bear us Christlike some bright winter
    morn!

This bright winter morn was realized for her in a special way on the day of her profession, on the feast of the Benedictine Oblate St. Frances of Rome:

I was allowed to make vows of poverty, chastity and obedience on March 9, 1944. "Beloved daughters, what do you wish?" my novitiate companions and I were asked that day in 1944 when we took our first vows in St. Frances Chapel in Baltimore. "Right Reverend Monsignor," we responded in unison, "the goodness of God has shown me the nothingness of this world and all that the world holds dear. I desire to consecrate myself to Jesus Christ, to serve Him with all my heart in this pious association of which I promise to observe the rules with an entire fidelity."

More than fifty years after the day of her first profession of religious vows, as she set out to found a new order of sisters, Sister Wilhelmina recalled these words of petition, declaring, "I desire that no less today."

Sister Wilhelmina made her final profession as an Oblate Sister of Providence on the feast of the Assumption, August 15, 1947. It was the same day on which St. Frances of Rome had made her consecration to Our Lady in 1425; it was also the thirtieth anniversary of the vow that her spiritual director, Fr. William Markoe, had made to devote his life to the service of the Black people. On that day in 1947, Sister Wilhelmina received a silver nuptial ring espousing her forever to Jesus Christ. Inscribed in her ring were the date and the simple initials "JMJF," signifying her devotion to Jesus, Mary, Joseph, and her special patroness, the Benedictine Oblate St. Frances of Rome.

7

Kaleidoscope Experience

Although Sister Wilhelmina relished her studies she soon found that the community apostolate of educating children was a very different experience. Life in the classroom was a challenge, teaching children from impoverished and often troubled backgrounds from the inner-cities of Baltimore, Washington, DC, St. Louis, Pennsylvania, Maryland, South Carolina, and Florida. Sister wrote:

> In September 1944, I was brought to the Motherhouse and assigned to work in the pantry. Soon after New Year's, I was given a fourth-grade class whose teacher was being transferred elsewhere. So my teaching career began, a kaleidoscope of good days and bad days that I was constantly praying to be delivered from. I loved study and school, but not teaching. During the 22 years between 1944 and 1966 I had a short, happy stint at housework—mainly cleaning—at St. Rita's Residence in St. Louis and then at St. Frances Home

for Girls where I learned that children had worries and broken hearts.

Her teaching days were not without excitement and even danger, especially in her inner-city classrooms. "I never stood up; I always sat while teaching," she recalled. Something inspired her, however, to stand up just as a troubled youth threw a knife that would have struck her in the eye. Since Sister Wilhelmina was rising, the knife missed her face and instead bounced off her stiff plastic wimple and fell harmlessly to the ground.

The mid-twentieth century brought many cultural changes and technological innovations, including television. Sister Wilhelmina was shrewd in her appraisal of this new means of communication and entertainment: "Television came into my life during the fifties when I was at St. Rita's, and I wondered how I had lived so many years without it. Recreation in the evening consisted in sitting down before it and listening to everything it had to say. After some years I was thoroughly disenchanted with it because one couldn't talk back to it but had to be completely on the receiving end, taking in both error and foolishness."

Sister Wilhelmina wrote years later that, in spite of her dislike for teaching, her love for the True Presence of Our Lord in the Eucharist was her primary motivator in entering the Oblate Sisters of Providence. Teaching about the Mass and sacraments proved to be a joy.

> Attendance at Mass took on a different aspect as I sat behind rows of squirming fourth-graders, some of whom were not Catholic. Like a mother hen hovering

over her brood, I was anxious—perhaps too anxious—
that they have the same regard for this awesome sacrifice as I had. I wanted the children to appreciate the
Mass and to get all possible benefit from it; but alas,
some of them were not even baptized. Was I expecting
too much? I sometimes wondered. In those days the
Ward method of teaching music was being introduced,
and one could step from it very easily into Gregorian
Chant. The grand accomplishment of a fourth-grader
before he passed into fifth was to sing Credo III. I
am amazed as I remember how much Latin the children learned and sang with seeming pride and satis-
faction. It was also my duty to teach the rudiments
of Latin pronunciation—mainly the necessary Mass
responses—to those fourth-grade boys who hoped to
become altar boys the next year. *Ad Deum qui laetificat
juventutem meam.* How proudly they would say the
words so that they could join the club! Faithful altar
boys were taken on special trips by the grateful pastor. While eighth-grade boys were cocks-of-the-walk
as altar boys, the eighth-grade girls were in demand as
a choir for funerals. They had a perfect mastery of the
Requiem Mass, including the Dies Irae, which they
sang as if they understood every phrase.

In August 1966, Sister Wilhelmina finished her bachelor
of arts degree, majoring in history, at the College of Notre
Dame of Maryland. The thesis that she submitted for her
degree had the arresting title "The Tragedy of Christianity,"
which she identified as the sad fact that "so much evil has

been done in the name of Christ," such as the oppression
and enslavement of entire peoples, and consequently that
the oppressed races have, for the most part, not received the
redemptive Blood of Christ, which He poured out for the
salvation of every race. In this paper, she showed herself to
be both a true daughter of Ella Madden Lancaster and a true
spiritual daughter of Mother Mary Lange in her zeal for the
evangelization of her people.

> Christ has been identified by many brown-skinned
> people of this planet as "the white man's God," hav-
> ing no concern for the black and coloured peoples of
> the earth. Yet Christ was born in Asia, and learned to
> walk in Egypt; it was upon African soil that Christ
> first set foot. It is strange that these two continents are
> still, majoritatively [sic] speaking, alienated from Him.
> It is the tragedy of Christianity that these millions of
> human beings, for whom He lived, suffered, taught
> and died, should live and die untaught, not knowing
> Him, enthralled in ignorance and moral degradation,
> blinded by the example of those who claim to have
> taught and to know, as well as by their own innate
> perversity, the heritage of the fall of Adam.

She understood that true freedom was the freedom of the
children of God, which was to be found only in the bosom
of Holy Mother Church. The path to this true freedom is
through enlightening the mind, for "those who refuse to
think are usually ruled by others who do their thinking for
them," she wrote. Once the mind is freed from ignorance,

then the will is freed to choose the good and to respond to the grace of faith.

> Faith is a free gift from God and can no more be forced upon anyone than a rosebud can be forced to open by violent pressure from without. . . . It was, and it still is, a great blessing to be a Christian, to be engrafted into a living, eternal organism, that is moving—like some planet in space—out of the trappings of time into the Parousia of eternity! True progress and betterment are assured for the individual who, gifted with the light of faith, freely elects to abide by the teachings and example of the Divine Master, and who thereby embraces the Christian commitment: to belong to Christ and to love all whom He loves, to be divinized, incorporated into Him as flesh of His flesh and blood of His blood, to be outcast no longer, to be elevated to a unique and eternal nobility, to be imbued with His Spirit, His Ideals, His very Life, and to be, thereby, saved. This is the viewpoint of faith.

Those who already possess the precious gift of faith have the grave responsibility to share this gift with others; thus she quotes St. Remigius, speaking to King Clovis when he ascended the throne, "With the riches left you by your father, ransom the captives and deliver them from the yoke of slavery." These words could be addressed to her own self, who received the riches of her Faith and her evangelical zeal from both her natural and her spiritual mothers.

After tracing the sad patterns of oppression through history, she comes to her own era, the societal upheaval of the 1960s. Here is the age of civil rights, of the Black man's coming into his own and into society, but at the same time here is the cultural revolution and society's wholesale abandonment of moral law. Hence Sister Wilhelmina concludes her thesis with the lament:

> Will the Black man ever be really free? Is there no other freedom for the Black man than the freedom which the devil offers? Freedom without God; freedom without integral family life; freedom without private ownership of property; freedom without freedom!
>
> You see, for so many centuries past, when our forebears were outcasts, the law stood pat. You know: "Thou shalt do thus" and "Thou shalt not do so." But now that we are winning our rights and making real headway into human society, all of a sudden nothing matters anymore. It is just as if a person skimped for years to buy himself a decent, up-to-date wardrobe, and finally, with the money in his fists, reached the store to find it closed.
>
> Come this way, Jesus Christ! Lord, stay with us, for our day is now just beginning. Others may be smart enough and self-sufficient enough to get along without you; but you must stay with us, for we will never let you go. We must keep you, because you're all we have; you are really *all* we have!"

What a vast difference there is, between suffering alone in pagan bondage, and suffering as the beloved of Christ, sustained and refreshed by His hidden manna!

Despite the provocative title, "The Tragedy of Christianity," Sister Wilhelmina did not consider the evil deeds of nominal Christians as cause for despair or for disillusionment with Holy Mother Church. Almost twenty years after submitting her thesis, Sister Wilhelmina wrote an epilogue for it, entitled "The Glory of Christianity" and typed on a piece of stationery with a picture of Mother Mary Lange and the oblates' motto, "Providence Will Provide." In this little essay, written on the feast of the Annunciation, March 25, 1985, she identified the paradoxical glory of the Catholic Faith:

> The glory of Christianity is that it requires all its adherents to be crucified along with their Master. "God forbid that I should glory save in the cross of Our Lord Jesus Christ by Whom the world is crucified to me and I to the world." Every man is born to live forever somewhere. Nobody wants to die, but die everyone must. . . . The good news is that we have been redeemed from sin by the Lord Jesus Christ. Yet we are not saved against our free wills: we must go along with Christ's program of prayer and penance according to our state of life and to the authentic direction of the Holy Spirit. No two souls are exactly alike in all respects. There is but one human race; each member of it, nonetheless, is unique, loved by God with an everlasting love.

8

The Winds of Change

The cultural revolution of the 1960s and 1970s had a great impact on her beloved community. They marked the most tumultuous epoch of Sister Wilhelmina's life personally, professionally, ecclesially, and communally. The changes in the Mass touched Sister Wilhelmina first and most profoundly. At St. Frances in Normandy, Missouri, she saw devotion tapering off.

> Again, sitting behind rows of girls, I wondered why there was so much lethargy; they were almost literally lying down in the pews, as if they had been out all night. I worried much over their couldn't-care-less attitude. Eventually, a gentleman seeing my concern, said, "Give 'em gospel." I hardly knew what "gospel" was then, and I was certain that it wasn't in the hymnbook we were using. For that matter, it wasn't in any of the music books that we were using. I soon learned that it was a style of music that didn't necessarily require adherence to written notes. One just sang or played

the way one felt, the louder the better. I also exper-
imented with the music of Ray Repp, writer of folk
songs for the Mass, and tried to make the Mass more
meaningful and appealing with: "Here we are! Altogether as we sing our song, Joyfully!" Neither "gospel"
nor the songs of Ray Repp solved the problem of Mass
attendance.

After the promulgation of the Novus Ordo Missae, the
New Missal of Paul VI on November 22, 1969, the Latin
Mass known for centuries before was swept away with a pen
stroke. Changes came with it: the addition of folk songs,
the priest facing the people to say Mass in English, recep-
tion of Communion on the hand, and the downplaying of
Our Lord's True Presence in the Blessed Sacrament to the
rank of being a mere "symbol" of Christ for many Catholics.
Observing all this, one elderly Sister commented to Sister
Wilhelmina, "Huh. I guess the Protestants were right!"

The sudden changes in the Oblate Sisters of Providence,
beginning with the religious habit, deeply upset Sister Wilhelmina. She tried to adapt to the initial stages of reform,
but she returned to the traditional habit a year after the
oblates had ceased using it altogether.

Improvement on the OSP Habit that began in the fifties and was completed in August 1962 I was happy
about; uniformity was desired by all the members of
the community, and this was a beautiful uniformity.
It lasted only five years. In January 1967 individual
Sisters were allowed to experiment with the headdress.
Hair-showing had begun. Of course I was not for

this at all. I had unfortunately gotten into that stupid hair-showing party; from June 1971 until Holy Saturday 1974 I was in it—to my great regret.

The rise of the "Black Power" movement, with its emphasis on African, sometimes pagan, cultural roots also affected the oblates. Initially, Sister Wilhelmina saw much hope in the movement, as she recounted: "In 1968 the National Black Sisters' Conference, begun by Sr. Martin de Porres Gray, RSM, gathered in Pittsburgh, PA, and forty-some OSP attended it. I was one of them, and I mistakenly believed that at last Catholic sisters were going to do something about the injustices towards Blacks so eloquently preached about by Rev. Martin Luther King, Jr., a Baptist minister. I disengaged myself from the NBSC in 1971 after their publication of 'Celibate Black Commitment' in which they stated that Blacks couldn't or shouldn't be celibate."

As she had expressed in her bachelor's thesis, Sister Wilhelmina understood that the true freedom and dignity of her race was the freedom and dignity of the children of God, the children of the Blessed Mother Mary, the children of Holy Mother Church. It is not the color of one's skin that matters but the purity of one's soul, as she explains in this following essay, written November 2, 1979, with its imaginative and thought-provoking plays on the word "black":

> There are those who say that there is no connection whatsoever between the Black Madonna of Poland and the so-called black people of the United States of

America and that black people look stupid venerating the Black Madonna of Poland as their Madonna.

I have news for them. Have you noticed the two scars on Our Lady's right cheek? Do you really know the story of how those scars got there? A Moorish soldier—yes, a colored man, one might say, from Northern Africa—slashed the picture twice with his sword, and dropped dead before he could land the third blow. He was angry because his side had lost the war against the Polish people, many years ago.

It is altogether fitting that descendants of Africans, that we, black or colored or Negro people as the world designates us, make up to the dear Mother of God and Mother of all men, as much as we can, with all possible love and devotion, for that insult offered to her so many years ago. It is true that Our Lady of Czestochowa is <u>not</u> black as we are; we are black, filthy sinners; but we love her just the same.

The 1970s were also a time of great change and transition in Sister Wilhelmina's personal life. Her teaching career came to an end in February 1972 after a student complained that Sister Wilhelmina had corrected her too severely. She related, "I was brought back to the Motherhouse in Baltimore, now newly built on Gun Road. For the first time in my life, the superior general, Sister Mary of Good Counsel Baptiste, asked me, breathing in exasperation, what I wanted to do. I immediately replied that I would like to write a history of the Order. That is how I got to work on archival material."

Sister Wilhelmina served as archivist for fourteen years and was also appointed extraordinary secretary to the General Chapter of 1973. She never did write a history of the Oblate Sisters of Providence, but she compiled valuable notes for such a document. Although she enjoyed her archival work, her transition from the classroom to the archives was not easy. She found her solace in submitting her writing talents to the service of her Beloved Lord:

> Around this time I became very despondent, feeling that I had failed as a teacher, that I could neither teach nor cook, and therefore why should I be alive. With my head on the desk in my cell, I was inspired with a poem honoring Our Lord in the Most Blessed Sacrament. When I finished writing it—and it came quite easily—I felt consoled and satisfied.
>
> I immediately took it to Sister Benigna who resided in the infirmary wing, but was still the community's topmost musician. She was not for any of the musical nonsense that was going on, and I knew that she would give my poem, "We Do Believe," quick shrift if that is what she thought it deserved. She read it, smiled, and then said, "I am going to write music for this." In a couple of weeks, it was done, and she was teaching it at choir practice. "We must not tell the Sisters where this hymn comes from, for they will not sing it then," she warned me.

Final contributors to Sister Wilhelmina's angst in the early 1970s were personal changes, and much closer to home.

These also brought Sister Wilhelmina to her "low point," when she had penned "We Do Believe." But Sister rallied again under the influence of Sister Benigna, along with her devotion to her natural and supernatural mothers.

Sister's parents endured a period of estrangement around this time, a pain Sister Wilhelmina only referred to in the years preceding her death. Soon after this mysterious period, tragedy struck. Oscar suffered from heart failure and passed away at a hospital in St. Louis. Sister Wilhelmina did not attend the funeral of her father, but she visited her mother afterwards. When Ella saw her daughter in the modified habit, she scowled and said to her daughter, "It is a good thing your father is not here to see you like that." She was then resolved to resume the traditional habit, the same that Sister Benigna had persevered in wearing. Sister Wilhelmina gave the final credit to her Beloved Blessed Virgin Mary: "Our Blessed Mother helped me put the traditional habit back on when her Pilgrim Virgin Statue of Our Lady of Fatima came to visit our Mount, and the sisters went in procession to the gate to meet it. Needless to say, my return to the habit was not just for that occasion, but for the rest of my life."

Sister made the habit herself, which required some ingenuity, especially as the oblates no longer made any of the parts. She ended up improvising the forehead piece of her wimple with a piece of plastic cut from a bleach bottle. A sister passing her in the hallway pointed at the traditional headdress and asked, "Are you going to wear that all the time?" "Yes!" Sister Wilhelmina was determined. As she would later quip, "I am Sr. Wil-hel-mi-na; I've a hell of a will and I mean it!"

9

Music and Memories

Sister Mary Wilhelmina served for fourteen years as archivist, in which time she not only attended to the historical documents of the community but also assisted other researchers. In 2004, Sister read aloud Father Michael Curley's biography of St. John Neumann to her new community. She was nearly finished with the book when a sister remarked on the closeness of the saint to the oblates, and that Father Curley must have had contact. Sister Wilhelmina, reticent as always to speak of any good she had done, admitted, "Yes, I knew him. I assisted him when he was doing research in Baltimore." Father Curley was also the author of a book on Francis Xavier Seelos that was also read by her sisters years later.

In December 1985, Sister Wilhelmina was appointed to assist Sister Benigna Holland in the Mount Providence Center of Music and General Culture. This was a happy assignment for her, which she enjoyed right up until the day in May 1995 when she left the Oblate Sisters of Providence to found a new traditional community. The two teamed up to write other hymns after their first collaboration, "We Do Believe." Sister Wilhelmina was especially devoted to her friend: "Sr. Benigna was like a mother to me in many ways. She was one of the few Oblates who persevered in wearing the traditional habit; she taught me much by example in my young days, and even more after I became her assistant. A concert pianist (and accompanist to Marian Anderson) before entering the Oblates in 1930, she also had high musical standards. It was she, for instance, who taught me Gregorian chant and pointed out the value of the *Liber Usualis*."

Under the tutelage of Sister Benigna, she also gained a deep appreciation for the musical patrimony of the Church. She began to see Ray Repp's "catchy, not churchy" dictum as a repudiation of the centuries of tradition that had come before. Sister Wilhelmina reflected:

> In the old days the music was straightforward in style and dogmatic in substance. Hymns reinforced Church teachings. There was reverence, awe, majesty in them. Nowadays music is relaxed, formless, focused on self. I spent my youth studying diligently, striving to learn standard English as well as music, and now I am expected to be delighted with dialect and cornfield ditties. At Mass I want to give God my best, which broken or infantile English is not, just as various aberrations have been embraced in the name of "the spirit of Vatican II," so there have been numerous vitiations of the Novus Ordo. When the Novus Ordo began, with its choices of prefaces and Eucharistic acclamations, I

had no idea that these would be bypassed for other expressions whenever there was felt to be a "need." I never dreamed that the beautiful Latin hymns and motets would be banned as "foreign to the culture" or "beyond the understanding" of the people.

In 2018, the last year of Sister Wilhelmina's life, she received a letter of thanks from a former student from this period. He had pursued a musical career, becoming the director of music for a Catholic parish in Florida, and was overjoyed to recognize Sister Wilhelmina's name in a community newsletter: "So often I look back on my musical studies with Sr. Benigna and yourself at the Mt. Providence motherhouse so many years ago. . . . I thank God daily for having your influence in my life."

While Sister Wilhelmina was going through these changes in her own life, her community continued to undergo experimentation, setting aside many traditional practices of religious life along with the habit. In response, Sister Wilhelmina wrote an essay entitled "Sister, Sister, Why Did You Enter?" It does not appear to have been published; perhaps she simply gave it to her fellow oblates to read. This paper eloquently expresses Sister Wilhelmina's understanding of her own vocation. She first identifies the purpose of religious life, in contrast to the notion in vogue that a religious was a social worker or a member of a sorority.

> To be a religious means to consistently and openly express a total love for Jesus Christ in a particular intimacy which is neither expected nor required of the

common Christian. A religious strives to be here on earth what all are destined to be in Heaven, totally engaged in Divine Union. The essence of religious living is neither apostolic concern nor the sharing of a common fellowship . . . the essential element of being a religious lies wholly in the realm of Divine grace obtained through assiduous prayer and the sacraments faithfully received.

Moreover, the total love for Jesus Christ is expressed in a <u>certain</u> poverty, a <u>certain</u> chastity, a <u>certain</u> obedience, and in the practice of all the Christian virtues. A religious is ever bent on getting to know Christ better through daily meditation on the Scriptures, and on empathizing with His every joy and pain.

Sister Wilhelmina encouraged her fellow religious to rise above the current class wars caused by discrimination and racism: "Anyone who would save his soul as a vowed religious of the Roman Catholic Church must, absolutely must, transcend all notions of class, caste and race, both from the 'oppressor-superior' viewpoint as well as from the 'victim-inferior' viewpoint. Both views are equally damaging to whoever harbors them."

She also addressed the prevalent prejudices against religious authority, in the face of a culture that would democratize the religious life, demanding independence, individual rights, self-determination and self-fulfillment, and casting suspicion and distrust between religious and their superiors: "God is able to write straight with crooked lines. . . . Observers should not mourn overmuch upon noticing inequities in the choice of superiors, although inequities in plenty there may be. Every religious in good spiritual health and in her right mind is truly happy to be obedient and subject, because the path of obedience is the safe and sure path; when one obeys, she is certain of doing God's will rather than her own."

She entertained no pretensions about the frailty and faults of religious, describing each as a weak and sinful soul who nevertheless "daily strives to cause joy among the angels of God in Heaven by the enactment of her own sincere conversion." For this, she must persevere in obedience to "the guidelines drawn up by ecclesial authority for the proper ordering of the religious Christian's life."

> Whenever a religious steps outside her cloister to fraternize with her brothers and sisters in the world, she is thereby presented with the odd and alluring opportunity of enjoying an extra, unscheduled, pizza and beer herself. Instead of criticizing religious as living in their ivory towers, insensitive to the world's needs, society really should be thankful that the bums are off the streets. The present-day demand that nuns come out of their cozy cloisters and socialize with the people has dubious origins. Part of the pressure might be the translation of a wonder how it is that religious can seemingly have such good times . . . and a desire to be invited to the conventual party as an observer of, and a partaker in, the joy.

They who choose a sacrificial life for the love of God are often endowed by God with manna of such unspeakable sweetness that even unbelievers can perceive that something marvelous is sustaining them in spite of their deprivations. But this manna God gives to all who seek Him sincerely, as He promises: "Seek first the Kingdom of God and His justice and all other things will be given you besides." God simply cannot be outdone in generosity, especially to those who have been so generous as to surrender themselves entirely to Him.

For many years, Sister Wilhelmina persistently petitioned her fellow oblates to allow her to start a traditional branch of the community, adhering more to the old practices and habit that had been put aside.

I had no thought or desire of leaving my community in those days, but I was gung-ho for seeing it reformed. We had made a wrong turn, I said, and should go back. The rule of silence and monthly chapter were long gone. Sisters were invited—I was working in the archives then—to submit a replacement or improvement of Chapter. I wrote something and handed it in but never heard anything of it. Something else that I wrote in December 1972, "Is There Light at the End of the Tunnel?" was presented at a community meeting and caused a stir. It suggested that OSP recognize themselves as a three-pronged venture, one of which would be a contemplative unit. My suggestion nettled those who wanted to see us give up the habit completely and go into all the lovely colors. Others who were not as far out as this nonetheless saw the contemplative life as something medieval, dangerous and unjust.

The Chapter of 1973 was an education for me. Although not an elected delegate, I was appointed an extra secretary, and I witnessed all that happened without being able to open my mouth. All OSP had been allowed to submit proposals to the Chapter, and I submitted mine that a contemplative unit be formed. In Chapter after Chapter—1973, 1977, 1985, 1989, under some wording or another, I submitted this idea. At last in 1993 I thought I had the perfect wording "traditional house be established" and this passed. It was hamstrung from the very beginning.

Sister Wilhelmina's proposal follows:

I, Sr. Mary Wilhelmina Lancaster, O.S.P., remembering my initial formation and early training as an Oblate Sister of Providence, desire to bolster the infrastructure of the practices of genuine religious life. I desire to pass on to others the traditional practices which formed the infrastructure:

The wearing of a uniform habit,
The surrendering of all monies to a common
    bursar,
The obeying of lawful authority in all
    departments,

The guarding of enclosure and of times and places
of silence,

And the living together [of] an authentic fraternal
life.

She then submitted the name of the only sister willing to embark on such a project: Sister M. Wilhelmina Lancaster, OSP.

Sister Wilhelmina had not been entirely bereft of support. Many sisters, especially from among the thirty-three community members who wore the traditional habit, expressed their personal backing for her initiative. But none felt that they could officially join her. Even Sister Benigna, who loved Sister Wilhelmina so much, sadly told her "I am too old." Sister Wilhelmina described the disappointing conclusion to her initiative: "Sr. Claudine Sanz, the superior general, announced to the whole community several months later, 'We are the traditional house.' Although humiliated, I was happy to be finished with the work of trying to reform the OSP. I saw nothing ahead of me but silent perseverance in the community until I died."

Cries to Peter

During this troubling time of isolation within her own community, between 1979 and 1993, Sister Wilhelmina had regular recourse to the Holy Father, Pope St. John Paul II. She first opened her heart to her Father in Rome in 1979, sending him her essays "Consider This" and "A Sesquicentennial Salute," sharing with him her love of her race and of her religious community, both of which she saw as needing true conversion and authentic reform. She wrote him several times subsequently, encouraging him and thanking him for his apostolic labors and sharing with him her own efforts to remain faithful to the apostolic tradition.

As experimentation within the oblates' community reached the liturgy, Sister Wilhelmina wrote, protesting the introduction of African-American rites and begging for a traditional ordinariate, as requested by Una Voce, a coalition for preserving the Latin Mass:

January 19, 1991

Most Holy Father:

I see no need for an African rite.

I see no need for an American rite.

I see no need for an African-American rite.

I adhere to the Roman rite. Latin is the official language of the Roman rite. Gregorian chant is the official music of the Roman rite.

I am a subject of Christ's kingdom, which is <u>not</u> of this world.

Our Lord Jesus Christ founded one Church for all men regardless of skin color, regardless of living conditions, regardless of mother tongue.

Everyone must die to himself and put on Christ. "Forget your people and your father's house," the psalm says.

Please, Holy Father, listen to the cry of Una Voce: Establish a Traditional Ordinariate Consecrated to the Immaculate Heart of Mary!

She followed this with a letter to Augustin Cardinal Mayer dated January 25, 1991, containing a single pithy statement: "I am determined to remain a strict Roman Catholic and to have nothing whatsoever to do with the so-called African-American Catholic Church."

Sister Wilhelmina also sent unauthorized translations of psalms and canticles to Rome, begging that the superiors not mandate these spurious versions for the community's usage: "May religious communities change the wording of psalms or of familiar prayers such as the doxology at their pleasure? Please respond." Cardinal Mayer responded in the negative; Sister Wilhelmina brought this document to the attention of the Oblate Chapter, proposing that all Oblate Sisters of Providence adhere to traditional prayer forms used by the rest of the Roman Catholic Church, as Cardinal Mayer's letter stipulated. Her proposal, however, was not seconded and thus died on the floor of the chapter.

Sister Wilhelmina, however, endured and even embraced these frustrations and heartaches as a purification. She shared this growth of her soul with the Holy Father; the formulaic replies from the papal secretary never dampened her vibrant faith in the pope's loving concern for her as his true spiritual daughter:

Ascension Thursday, 1991

Most Holy Father:

Thank you for all your prayers and sacrifices for me! I have changed—my outlook has changed, become more Christian, more united with the Hearts of Jesus and Mary—since I first wrote you in 1979. You must have prayed for me!

I am sorry for any trouble that I caused you in 1979 with my ignorance and selfishness. Today I witness, even when I must stand alone: To be <u>black</u> is <u>nothing</u>! To be <u>Catholic</u> is <u>everything</u>!

Thank you again, my dear suffering, hard-working Holy Father! I will be remembering you in prayer on your birthday, Saturday, May 18, the vigil of Pentecost.

Your loving daughter in Christ,
Sr. M. Wilhelmina Lancaster, O.S.P.

Sister Wilhelmina was able to see Pope St. John Paul II in person on the occasion of his visit to the Basilica of the National Shrine of the Immaculate Conception in Washington, DC, on October 7, 1979. The purpose of his visit was to deliver a major address to women religious, which Sister Wilhelmina gladly attended. Sadly, at the conclusion of the pope's address, a religious sister delivered her own remarks in which she admonished the Holy Father for upholding the Church's teaching that women cannot be ordained priests. Sister Wilhelmina was indignant and wrote a formal letter of apology to St. John Paul II on behalf of all the women religious in attendance, and she received a reply from the secretariat of state.

She also had a personal encounter with St. John Paul II some years later, after she had left the Oblates of Providence to found a traditional community. In the late 1990s, she had the opportunity to travel to Rome with her new sisters and attend a papal audience. Because her age required her to use a wheelchair during this pilgrimage, she was given a place in the front row and even brought forward to greet the pope. She clasped his hand and exclaimed with joy, "Thank you, Holy Father, thank you, thank you!" This encounter with Christ's representative remained one of her favorite memories.

Sister Wilhelmina's final extant letter to Rome is addressed to Joseph Cardinal Ratzinger as head of the Congregation for the Doctrine of the Faith, in which she shares with him another unauthorized paraliturgical rite used by the oblates for the feast of the Immaculate Conception. She further shares with him seven points that she was resolved to follow in regard to her perseverance "as a Roman Catholic in sanctifying grace and as a true religious and child of the Blessed Virgin Mary." Her points are as follows:

1. I am not interested in leaving my community and founding another.
2. I see a rich spiritual patrimony, a Roman Catholic spirituality, as belonging to us Oblate Sisters of Providence.
3. Specifically, our Roman Catholic spirituality is Total Consecration to Jesus through Mary, and devotion to Our Lord Jesus Christ truly present in the Most Holy Sacrament of the Altar.
4. Social upheaval and misrepresentation of the Documents of Vatican II have obscured this, our patrimony, from us.
5. Consequently, I propose, I urge, the establishment of a traditional house: so that our spiritual patrimony may be secured and made to live again, unmolested by the spirit of this passing world.
6. The security of our traditional lifestyle must be guaranteed by persons of like mind regarding the essentials of it coming together in one place, not merely talking about it, but actually living the traditional life.

7. Only if such agreement cannot be reached will it be necessary to appeal to the Pope for a new foundation.

She concluded, "Please, Your Eminence, help me to save my soul according to the Will of Almighty God." The moment for the new foundation was at hand.

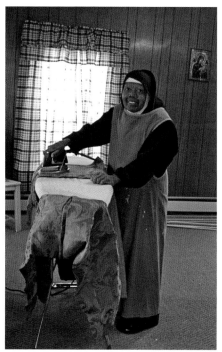

11

Bag and Baggage

Sister Wilhelmina had been regularly attending the Latin
Mass in the late 1980s and early 1990s at St. Alphon-
sus Church in Baltimore and Old St. Mary's in Washington, DC. Both were former Redemptorist parishes where
the Latin Mass was allowed to continue. She wrote of this
decision:

> I have finally come to my senses. I am resolved to return
> to the traditional Latin Mass, so that I can pray to God
> without distraction. In the old days, before the Novus
> Ordo, my eyes were always wide open as I watched
> the mysterious, endlessly fascinating actions of the
> priest. With the Novus Ordo, I find myself sometimes
> obliged to close my eyes so that I can't see the priest.
> In the old days my neighbor seemed just as intent as I
> was in watching the altar. Now my neighbor seems to
> be focused on me, and the others around him. I never
> could stand the hand-shaking, hugging and kissing
> that goes on just before Communion. Out of sheer

justice and charity there should be, at all Novus Ordo Masses, some portion of the church reserved for the use of persons who do not care to exchange greetings during Mass. Kissers and huggers should stay out of the area and not molest the persons there.

Don't get me wrong. I have always been a supporter of active participation at Mass. For years before Vatican II, I did my utmost to promote the Missa Recitata. But I have also long appreciated the fact that the Mass is public, liturgical prayer, which differs from private, personal prayer. When one prays privately he can use any words, any books, any posture, any time. There are no rules, no rubrics. But for the Mass, everything is prescribed, because the liturgy is the prayer of not just the local community, but the entire Roman Catholic Church, the entire Mystical Body of Christ. That is why, for liturgy, the question of "approved texts" is fundamental. Liturgical norms allow—and even encourage—a priest to vary the wording of greetings in the Mass, and to give explanations at certain fixed points. But the wording of the prayers, readings—and above all the Eucharistic prayers—is to be as set down in the approved texts only. So I'm frankly fed up with all the ad-libbing that goes on nowadays in the Mass. In my opinion, the worst confusion since the promulgation of the Novus Ordo has resulted from this substituting of personal prayer for the liturgy, which has literally driven some people out of the assembly. And now, as if things weren't already bad enough, a campaign is underway to change the existing English translations of both the Novus Ordo Mass as well as the Divine Office, to make them more "inclusive" of women. What nonsense. Anyone without sufficient grasp of our language to understand that women are, and always have been included in such terms as "mankind," has no business correcting third-grade English papers, much less the language of the liturgy. But enough—enough!—of these musical hacks, these illiterate improvisers, these tireless revisers, these liturgical lobbyist who treat the Mass as if it were their personal propaganda tool. At long last, I am going back to the tried and the true, to the set and unchanging—to the traditional Latin Mass.

Two days after the consecration of four bishops without ecclesiatical approbation, John Paul II released the Motu Proprio *Ecclesia Dei* in 1988. Along with the condemnation of the act and excommunications (subsequently lifted by Pope Benedict), the letter went on to address the bishops and the entire Church. It was this in particular that Sister Wilhelmina declared to be "news that I latched onto as salvific. I was determined to return to and attend the Traditional Latin Mass as much as possible." The consecration had opened a deeper awareness of faithful souls like Sister Wilhelmina who were longing for a return to tradition within the Church at large. The Motu Proprio stated:

> To all those Catholic faithful who feel attached to
> some previous liturgical and disciplinary forms of the
> Latin tradition I wish to manifest my will to facilitate

their ecclesial communion by means of the necessary measures to guarantee respect for their rightful aspirations. In this matter I ask for the support of the bishops and of all those engaged in the pastoral ministry in the Church. . . .

Respect must everywhere be shown for the feelings of all those who are attached to the Latin liturgical tradition, by a wide and generous application of the directives already issued some time ago by the Apostolic See for the use of the Roman Missal according to the typical edition of 1962.

Sister Wilhelmina made many friends among the traditional Catholics of Baltimore. They facilitated her annual retreats in 1991 with the Sisters of Charity of Mary Mother of the Church in Baltic, Connecticut, and in 1992 with the Slaves of the Immaculate Heart of Mary in Still River, Massachusetts. In the course of this latter retreat, Sister Wilhelmina happened to meet Sister Therese McNamara. Sister Therese was just about to leave the Slaves of the Immaculate Heart to join the traditional Benedictine community in Le Barroux, France.

Sister Therese, born Deidre McNamara, entered the Slaves of the Immaculate Heart at only fourteen years of age. She proceeded to make her novitiate with the Slaves, professing perpetual vows in 1981. Sister Wilhelmina remembered their first encounter: "Something told me then that the young Sister Therese who was directing the music at Mass that August 22nd would be my superior some day. 'See that sister down there?' she heard inside. 'She's going to be your Superior some day.' I rejected the idea as impossible and unreasonable. 'That little thing? No way!' But the voice finished, 'You'll see, and when it happens, you will know the truth of this.'"

Sister Wilhelmina finished her retreat and returned to the Oblate Sisters of Providence and her hoped-for renewal. She did, however, remain in contact with Sister Therese, recognizing their shared aspirations for the resurgence of traditional religious life.

Sister Wilhelmina's personal notes during these years, 1993–1995, reveal the struggle in her soul as she sought to discern whether to persevere unto death in the order to which she had been faithful for more than fifty years or to start anew. She had recourse, as always, to the Blessed Mother of God:

March 13, 1994

Because I want to persevere in the one true faith and witness for it, please help me to break whatever human ties I must in order to do so as a true religious and your most devoted child.

The following day, March 14, she drafted a letter to a priest of the newly formed Fraternity of St. Peter, whom she had heard was interested in forming a traditional group of religious sisters: "Although I have been professed fifty years as an Oblate Sister of Providence, I am ready to begin anew serving Mother Church, having no desire whatsoever of being relieved of my perpetual vows but rather to persevere as a true religious and child of Mother Mary. Please let me know what is going on."

On March 18, she composed a prayer to the Holy Ghost: "Lord Holy Spirit, Creator Blest, guide me in my quest for true religious life. For fifty years I have been an Oblate Sister of Providence. Help me to persevere as a Roman Catholic. The chapter approved the proposal 'that at least one traditional house be established.' Although no Oblate has been found to join me, help me to move out from among the Oblate Sisters as I should and work for the establishment of traditional sisters under the aegis of the Priestly Fraternity of St. Peter."

Three days later, March 21, saw the addition of a simple resolution: "I will willingly put beneath my feet all ethnic ties, and all self-aggrandizement, so as to be with You and Your Church totally, dying with You, so that I can rise again with You! While suffering here, I look forward to the joys of Heaven!" And two days later, she added the plea, "Lord Jesus, help me as a true religious to surrender all attachment to my ethnic origin. You were rejected by your people, the Jews, and handed over to the Romans. Yet You loved Your people dearly. Ridiculed as "King of the Jews," You became the Savior of the World. Help me to humbly follow You, the Good Samaritan, the Nazarene, my Beloved."

At the end of the summer of 1994, Sister Wilhelmina wrote a poem reflecting on her fifty years in vows as an Oblate Sister of Providence. She borrowed an image from Pharaoh's dream, which the patriarch Joseph interpreted to mean years of plenty followed by years of famine (see Gn 41), to express the changes that she underwent in her religious life. Her "temptations, attempts and failures," how-ever, she recognized as part of the Lord's loving providence for her. Even amid the anxiety and frustration, alluded to in "long, hot, sleepless nights," she recognized her trials as a purification for herself and ultimately a source of union with God in "deep delights of prayer."

Around this time of interior struggle, Sister Wilhelmina learned of the arrival of the Priestly Fraternity of St. Peter in Scranton, Pennsylvania, from Wigratzbad, Germany. She went with friends in a van to attend fraternity events such as the solemn dedication of St. Gregory's Chapel in Elm-hurst. John Ambs, the driver of the van on that trip, knew about the failure of Sister Wilhelmina's 1993 proposal to the OSP Chapter. During the drive from Scranton, he informed Sister Wilhelmina that Sister Therese McNamara had come to Elmhurst. "Oh, no," Sister Wilhelmina replied. "She has gone to join a traditional community in France." "But she is back!" John replied. How he knew is a mystery, for the day that he spoke with Sister Wilhelmina was the same day that Sister Therese flew back to the United States. He suggested that the two sisters spearhead a new traditional community. Sister Wilhelmina stated, "I did not hesitate." She wrote immediately to Sister Therese:

April 27, 1995

My last letter to you, Sr. Therese, was in June of last year, and in it I said that I had been strongly tempted to leave my community so as to join or form another, but that I had thought that temptation was over. Well, it's back, stronger than ever. Does God *really* want me to come to Scranton to join you? Such seems to be the case. I am actually praying now that God *will help me to leave* the Oblate Sisters of Providence of which I have been a professed member since 1944 and to join you in Scranton!

Imagine! Lord, not my will but Thine be done. . . . I'm praying the Miraculous Medal Novena not only for the needs of the Priestly Fraternity of St. Peter, but also the formation of—let us say—the Religious Sorority of St. Benedict. Ut in Omnia [sic] Deus glorificetur.

Sister Anna Marie McCormack, a Benedictine of Corpus Christi Monastery in Michigan, had also come to Elmhurst with the blessing of her superior. She had aided Sister Therese upon her return to America, and had begun a proposal for a new community. Sister Wilhelmina also wrote to Sister Anna Marie after Easter, asking if she would be the foundress and emphasizing the need for clear authority from the start. Sister Wilhelmina summarized a future vision: "You want independently governed sisters, yet sisters who walk parallel with the Priestly Fraternity of St. Peter, attending the traditional Latin Mass daily, and doing all in their power to spread it. This of course certainly means educating the young in Latin and Gregorian chant as well as praying in these ourselves. We should teach our own membership before endeavoring to teach outsiders."

The letters addressed to Sister Therese and Sister Anna Marie were both shown to Father Devillers, who wrote to Sister Wilhelmina on May 4, 1995. He invited her to come for a visit, proposed St. Gregory's Priory in Scranton as a possible first location of a new order of sisters, and told her of Bishop Timlin's approval of this new community. "I believe we might be able to begin this Summer or Fall," he wrote, "with your assistance." In closing he said, "We need your experience!"

She did indeed take the decisive step: exactly one month later, she left her beloved oblates "bag and baggage," as she would frequently say later, setting off upon the new and mysterious path to which the Lord was calling her. With the blessing and permission of her superiors, she bade farewell to her sisters. Most difficult was her goodbye to her beloved guide and mentor. She later wrote: "Leaving Sr. Benigna, and all the rest of my fellow Oblates, was like leaving home a second time. They, like my parents and family, made me what I am today. I have many good memories of them, especially those early years when holy silence, much communal prayer, communal reading and wearing the habit were still important and practiced by all."

Sister Wilhemina recalled the remainder of that historic day: "It was Mr. Ambs who collected the near one thousand dollars for my entry into the aegis of the FSSP and presented it, along with my arrival May 27, 1995 to Fr. Arnaud Devillers, FSSP."

Fr. Arnaud Devillers's intention in establishing the new community of Oblate Sisters was to answer the need for traditional active sisters to assist the Priestly Fraternity of St. Peter in their parish work. Several sisters from other communities had approached Father Devillers in the hope of founding such a community, but as he recounted years later,

"Sr. Wilhelmina impressed me the most—by far." He recognized her stable religious formation, her genuine humility and devotion, and also the experience that comes with age. Consequently, he judged her to be the ideal candidate to start "the Fraternity's sisters" in answer to "many requests in the past from girls and young ladies who were looking for a traditional and orthodox community of sisters." He appointed Sister Wilhelmina as the superior of the fledgling community, and wrote: "It's a question of finding the right people to begin with. And Sister Wilhelmina has been recommended to me for a long time. . . . They're definitely going to base their spirituality and rule on the rule of St. Benedict. Of course, Benedictine sisters are usually contemplative, but they're going to try to combine contemplative and active . . . teaching catechism to the children, helping in the sacristy work, taking care of the girls . . . not necessarily hav[ing] to work with priests of the Fraternity."

Sister Wilhelmina formulated a checklist for future postulants:

> We need subjects who . . .
>
> 1. Will give themselves entirely to Jesus through Mary.
>
> 2. Are determined to live a more perfect life, to avoid all that displeases God and to do all that God desires of them.
>
> 3. Esteem and love obedience as an excellent, necessary and useful virtue, and zealously observe the stipulations of our constitution regarding it.

4. Esteem and love poverty as the bulwark of religious life, the foundation of perfection, and zealously observe the stipulations on our constitution regarding it.

5. Value and esteem the works of charity in which the community engages, and in regard to sisterly love strive to follow the example of Christ expressed: "This is My commandment, that you love one another as I have loved you."

6. Zealously strive for humility, the moral virtue without which no other can exist, and really believe that they will never attain the aim of their holy vocation if they do not do their best to destroy self-love.

7. Strive to imitate the meekness of Jesus, and esteem and love prayer as an essential obligation, a necessary means without which the graces needed to fulfill the duties of their vocation cannot be obtained.

8. Have a boundless trust in God, expecting all from Him for themselves as well as for others.

9. Consider silence as one of the important points of the constitution and uphold the having of a reserved area.

10. Read, meditate on and sincerely strive to live by the gospel of our Lord Jesus Christ and the community's constitution.

Sister Wilhelmina had unwittingly described her own virtues, which she generously rendered to God in her "fiat" for a new foundation.

12

The Ship Leaves Shore

In an article entitled "Starting Over," published in the spring 1996 issue of *Sursum Corda*, Sister Wilhelmina described this turning point in her religious life:

> It would seem I've done a very foolish thing. After fifty years as an Oblate Sister of Providence I am starting the religious life anew—as foundress of a new community affiliated with the Priestly Fraternity of St. Peter. We will serve them in their own apostolate of offering Mass and the sacraments according to the traditional Latin rite, in conformity with the Holy Father's *motu proprio* 'Ecclesia Dei.' To those who say that my leaving my old community to found a new one doesn't make sense, I reply that it is understandable only in the light of faith.

She went on to describe the spiritual inspiration and the purpose that she envisioned for the new community: it would have a Marian character, seeking to be for the priests of our day what Our Lady was for the apostles during her earthly life. Just as Our Lady supported the apostles with her prayers and sacrifices and also with the work of her hands, making vestments and providing a home for them, so also these new oblates would assist the present-day apostles through their work and prayer.

There is a window in St. Gregory's Chapel in Elmhurst [at the Headquarters of the Priestly Fraternity] showing eleven apostles gathered around Our Blessed Mother during the nine days between Ascension Thursday and Pentecost Sunday. The Latin inscription on the wall around the picture reads: *Erant Discipuli Perseverantes Unanimiter In Oratione Cum Maria, Matre Jesus, Alleluia* (The disciples were persevering together in prayer with Mary the Mother of Jesus. Alleluia). This is a perfect description of the religious sisterhood that is now forming. Only the Apostles and Mary are seen in the picture; but Scripture tells us that many more *persons—discipuli—*were gathered in that building waiting for the coming of the Holy Spirit. Likewise, we Sisters work behind the scenes: through Mary, with Mary, in Mary, for Mary, trying to do for the Church today what she did during the years between the Ascension of her Son Jesus and her own Assumption. Mary helped the Apostles to live peacefully as brothers; she offered them the warmth and comfort of a place to stay and to offer the Holy Sacrifice; she gave them courage to go forth and teach all nations despite numerous obstacles. Like Mary, we Sisters work and pray for priests. We are active-contemplative, doing all in our power to further the Faith, in obedience to the Pope. We are zealous that the Mass be celebrated worthily, in accordance with time-honored tradition, throughout the world, for all men of all time.

Over twenty years later, when this article had been long forgotten and Sister Wilhelmina herself was too old to take part in the discussion, the sisters with one mind and heart chose this passage from the Acts of the Apostles, *Perseverantes Unanimiter In Oratione*, as the motto for their community, now an abbey. A year after this choice, the sisters discovered the article with their beloved foundress's vision for their community, a providential confirmation of what her community had become.

Within a few days of the founding, Sister Anna Marie could see that even with Sister Wilhelmina's experience, there were incompatible characters and visions among her subjects. There had been unfortunate misunderstandings of Sister Anna Marie's former commitments. She therefore took her leave of the new community, not without a valuable contribution to its beginning, and took up teaching at a fraternity apostolate.

Sister Wilhelmina embraced the new challenge of starting a religious community with her customary determination and spirit of prayer. In a note dated November 4, 1995, First Saturday, Sister Wilhelmina expressed the pillars of prayer upon which she hoped to build the community: "I strive to establish Oblates of Mary, Queen of Apostles. Praying the

Rosary and Way of the Cross together is a good practice for a day of recollection."

Upon this foundation of prayer, the oblates based their active apostolate. An article entitled "What *Do* the Sisters Do All Day," published in the fraternity's February 1996 newsletter, presents the way of life that Sister Wilhelmina had established for the sisters in just nine months. The structured day, alternating between periods of prayer and manual work, already anticipated a Benedictine way of life. The holy silence and spirit of prayer and self-sacrifice that had formed Sister Wilhelmina as a young Oblate of Providence now transformed the tediousness of the humble daily tasks of the new oblates:

> The steps from the sisters' work room on the third floor to the laundry room in the basement are many and steep and the loads are heavy; the stains and wrinkles are stubborn and the starch messy; the sacristy supply ordering is often quite hectic; the grinding of materials to make incense is noisy and monotonous; sewing with great precision for long periods on black fabric hurts the eyes. But there are holy priests to be formed here, a nation to be re-evangelized. There's a traditional and respectful liturgy to be restored, the Catholic Faith to be preserved, souls to be saved through the ministry of the priesthood. The spirit of silence in which we work permits us to ponder these things in our hearts, in union with Our Lady, who spent the last years of her earthly existence in the prayerful support

and assistance of the first priests and apostles of the
early Church.

One of Sister Wilhelmina's poems from these early days of
the Oblates of Mary, Queen of Apostles, expresses in verse
the preeminence of the contemplative aspect of the sisters'
way of life:

> Love is the law, the law supreme,
> Your inner principle of life;
> Christ is your Spouse;
> you are His wife.
> The inner life
> must be the soul
> Of all your outward
> self-control.

Because of her own single-hearted fidelity to her vocation,
Sister Wilhelmina sought similar dedication and determination from the sisters gathering around her. To one religious,
who after much vacillation finally asked to enter the community, provided that the spirituality and way of life were
not yet fixed, Sister Wilhelmina replied firmly, "The ship has
sailed." She knew too well that a soul without a determined
will could not make the commitment that religious consecration requires.

The task of leading a brand-new community, difficult for
any person at any age, was particularly so for Sister Wilhelmina, who had never been in a leadership role in her pre-
vious community and was also advanced in age.

As the first year of the oblates progressed, she took an

honest assessment of her limitations and her ability to continue to lead the oblates as she approached the end of her own life. Consequently, she humbly requested that Sister Therese take responsibility as superior. Father Devillers approved this change on March 2, 1996.

The change in leadership dramatically changed the course of the Oblates of Mary. Sister Wilhelmina had collaborated with Father Devillers to found a community of parish helpers to support the priests of the Fraternity, whereas Sister Therese had her own vision of a contemplative-active community that would include both the contemplative life she had experienced in the great Benedictine abbeys of France as well as the active apostolate with which she had been formed with the Slaves of the Immaculate Heart. Father Devillers counselled her that she could not have both; one aspect, either contemplative or active, would have to predominate. Sister Therese's strong personality, however, coupled with the serious privations in her own formation, prevented her from seeing that her ideal could not be lived in reality. By 1997, it was clear to all parties that her independent vision would make cooperation between the fraternity and the oblates unsustainable; the following year, the fraternity seminary moved to Nebraska, and the Oblates of Mary relocated to another area of the Scranton diocese.

The needful separation from the fraternity to pursue a monastic path ironically led to a struggle for stability. Numerous moves followed, as did a succession of temporary chaplains.

In 1998, Sister Wilhelmina almost parted with the community as well, but for a different reason and destination. In early June, just as the community was finishing prayer, the sisters began to process out of their little chapel at St. Gregory's Priory. Sister Wilhelmina rose from her seat and collapsed in the aisle. She was hospitalized for ten days with pneumonia, complicated by her fall and yet another one at the hospital while she was unattended. It was believed that she would not recover, so the newly-ordained Fr. Joseph Portzer, FSSP, was summoned to administer last rites. Sister Wilhelmina rallied immediately after the sacrament was conferred and went on to live another twenty-one years.

13

Sisters on the Move

The year 2000 was greeted amidst moving boxes, as the sisters had begun a chain of relocations in northeastern Pennsylvania. Sister Wilhelmina's writings and poetry of this time took all the inconveniences in stride, but heavily emphasized the need for future stability. Thankfully, the first persevering vocations entered in this year, both being admirers of monastic life. This was aided in part by the community's visits to Clear Creek in Oklahoma, toward which another move was contemplated. The documentation for possible relocation submitted to Bishop Edward Slattery was the fortuitous source of Sister Wilhelmina's hidden short autobiography, from which many unknown details of her early life were later drawn. The Oklahoma plan did not materialize, as the abbot of Fongombault anticipated hurdles at that particular time.

The kind abbot had prudently foreseen that the clarity of vision and monastic maturity the community needed could not be supplied by the monks. It could only be achieved by a firm internal resolution to definitively and independently embark on a monastic course in a clear self-understanding, unhindered by another community's influence or the admixture of apostolic labors. The abbot encouraged the sisters to find land and settle where they knew they were welcome: the Diocese of Scranton. The sisters settled on farmland just south of the New York border in Starrucca, Pennsylvania. The rural location and first semblance of stability brought great relief to the soul of Sister Wilhelmina, as did the five more persevering vocations that entered there.

During this time, Sister Wilhelmina had a crisis in her own religious life; in 2003, she was recalled to the Motherhouse of the Oblates of Providence. In June 1998, when her three-year exclaustration expired, she had written the oblates, "I will no longer continue on as an Oblate Sister of Providence." She concluded, "They never answered that letter." Then in 2003, after five years on the new foundation, she wrote the bishop of Scranton, requesting formally, and with her customary sense of rhythm, to make final vows in her new community: "The best, and really only, reason that I can give for allowing me to make final, perpetual, Benedictine vows is to permit God to continue his multitudinous, marvelous miracles and mercies."

However, in September 2003, she received a letter from the Vatican sending her back to the motherhouse in Baltimore to request dispensation from perpetual vows. She left the Oblates of Mary not knowing when, or even if, she would return.

It was bittersweet to see her motherhouse and her sister oblates after eight years. While she had many heartwarming reunions, she also could see clearly her inability to live according to the community's new ways. Sister Wilhelmina, holding fast to her initial formation, and the Oblates of Providence, continuing post-Vatican II experimentation, had grown in different directions. The emphasis on the community's African-American heritage led one oblate to remark, "You're Black first, and Catholic second." To this, Sister Wilhelmina declared what she had also written to the Holy Father: "To be black is nothing. To be Catholic is everything."

Sister continued to reflect at her motherhouse:

> What are Oblates witnessing? Is it wonderful blackness? Or the wonders of the Second Person of the Blessed Trinity, True God and True Man, Who said, "Without Me, you can do nothing." Oblates like to sing, "We've come this far by faith." This faith is in whom? And in what?
>
> God is not impressed, nor influenced in any way, by either "blackness" or "whiteness." God is just. He became man in time, was born of the Virgin Mary, in order to suffer and die for every human being born on this earth.

Sister Wilhelmina especially missed the silence in which her new community was immersed. She wrote on her sojourn:

> Last night at 9:45 since my next-door neighbors were still going strong in conversation, I got out of bed to

sit at my desk and to begin writing what may be called a treatise on silence:

"The most important thing in community living is the observance of holy silence. We are supposed to be living a life of prayer, and we need silence on our part so that God can get a word in.

There are 24 hours in a day. For a religious, most of these hours must be hours of silence. During the night, they are hours of Grand Silence, so that the soul can really hear what God has to say at the end of each day. Not everyone awakens on this side of eternity the next morning."

Sister Wilhelmina understood that external practices such as wearing the habit and observing silence were not ends in themselves nor guarantees of salvation, but simply safeguards for her vocation, her intimate relationship with Christ. She also understood that without these safeguards, she could easily lose her awareness of this consecration. She consequently renewed her resolve to maintain traditional religious observance:

I recognize that not all those who wear the habit persevere as religious, that the just man falls seven times a day, and that death is the end of all regardless of its manner. Perseverance in faith, hope and charity is important, and we must pray continually, asking for the salvation that Christ has won for us. Never, on this side of the grave, can we relax and say, "I need not fight any more."

I testify here in answer to the question: "Sr. Wilhelmina, after fifty and more years with the Oblate Sisters of Providence, at your age, why are you leaving them now?"

"I am a weak, human being, one of the 'poor, banished children of Eve.' I need holy silence Oblate Sisters of Providence do not provide. We are too mixed up with the laity here. We seem to put man (whom we see) before God (Whom we do not see)."

The distressing visit had an unexpectedly short duration: after just ten days, Sister Wilhelmina was allowed to return to the Oblates of Mary, Queen of Apostles. Her faithful friends Kelly and Christine Mucker brought her to Starrucca, where her sisters had prepared a fried chicken supper, Sister Wilhelmina's favorite. When the sisters asked if she wanted seconds, Sister Wilhelmina bashfully confessed that the Muckers had likewise treated her to fried chicken for lunch. In November, the termination of her status with the Oblates of Providence was finalized, and she was able to renew her vows in her new community the following year, August 22, 2004.

The long-awaited stability found in Starrucca was also of unexpectedly short duration. Bishop Timlin had graciously initiated the Oblates of Mary, Queen of Apostles, but only as a "pious union." In 2005, his successor, Bishop Joseph Francis Martino, noted that the community had never been erected as a novitiate, and had therefore not received a canonical formation. Now that Sister Wilhelmina had been released from her vows, formation had to be given by a non-member so that status of a public association could be granted. A long search followed, but all plans fell through. One superior general said of the situation, "You know what I call this? A sanctoral mess! You might be better off just starting over."

In the diocese, the new bishop began the work of merging parishes. Scranton was full of churches built closely together, each serving an ethnic group. Not only had faith decreased and ethnic ties fizzled, the population had almost halved in seventy-five years. Amidst the mergings, the bishop's solution for the community ran along a similar vein: to be incorporated into another community. As this would have required the adoption of new usages and liturgy, the community appraised the earlier suggestion of the superior general, in light of a summons to Missouri.

14

Back in Missouri

The Oblates of Mary received an invitation from Bishop Robert Finn to his diocese of Kansas City-St. Joseph, Missouri in early 2006; he had been praying to find a community of sisters who would pray and sacrifice for his priests. In March, he warmly welcomed the small community of fourteen sisters to his diocese.

Throughout all these transitions, beginning with the change in leadership in 1996 and culminating with a move halfway across the country, the sisters were struggling to understand their own charism and purpose, and to realize Sister Therese's vision of being all-contemplative and all-active at the same time and with the same intensity. As they realized more and more their Benedictine identity, they changed their name from the Oblates to the Benedictines of Mary, Queen of Apostles; they received the necessary formation from Conception Abbey, a few hours north of Kansas City, and renewed their vows as full-fledged Benedictines.

Conflict persisted, however, between "being," as contemplative Benedictines, and "doing," as active religious sisters. Claiming and carrying responsibility for the community's foundation, Sister Therese providentially steered the community toward the contemplative Benedictine life, corresponding with the graces God gave her. There was, nevertheless, a lack of internal stability in those days as a balance was still sought.

During these difficult years, Sister Wilhelmina's stability was the community's foundation. She had, thankfully, greatly underestimated her own strength when she had requested to be relieved of the burden of office; not only did she persevere for twenty-three more years of religious life, but she remained an inspiration to the far-younger women who joined the little community. One novice recalled that when she doubted her own ability to persevere under the difficult circumstances, she looked to Sister Wilhelmina, peacefully ironing the traditional white wimple. She thought, "Yes, I can persevere in this life as she has."

Another sister, who was crying over a difficulty she faced in those early years, was discovered by Sister Wilhelmina. She warmly embraced the sister, saying soothingly, "Aw, baby doll!" Without another word, they returned to work. It was just enough for them both to take up their daily cross once more. For another novice, who was evidently also experiencing a trial, Sister Wilhelmina left a tender poem that reflected her charity toward her sisters and also her lively faith in God's ability "to write straight with crooked lines:"

> My little one,
> God's will be done,
> For both you and me.

You'll be a saint,
Without complaint,
Just you wait and see!

This was the faith that Sister Wilhelmina lived. When she herself recieved a harsh correction, she humbly composed a poem in response:

I want to do what God wants,
Please tell me what to do!
I'm sorry for my worrying—
My lack of trust in you.

Please give me one more chance to be
Your Oblate Sister true
In God I trust! In God I trust!
And so I trust in you.

In spite of her positive outlook, the strain of the foundational years began taking its toll on Sister Wilhelmina. She began to have increasingly frequent seizures. She also grieved to see sisters leave, some after struggling for years to preserve their vocations. Sister admitted that after "someone I loved very much left," she realized how serious a crisis the community was suffering.

The long-term effects of the conflict of ideals became apparent, Sister Therese resigned from her post and took leave of the community in July 2010. In her place, the bishop appointed Mother Cecilia Snell as prioress. Mother Cecilia would lead the community to a lasting home in Gower, Missouri, where construction had already begun on a guest house that the sisters were to live in temporarily. Later, prudence dictated that it become the monastery, which was made possible by future additions and the abbatial church.

Mother Cecilia and each of these sisters who entered before 2010 attest to the powerful example and influence of Sister Wilhelmina's fidelity on their individual perseverance. Her poetry reflected not only her trusting serenity in the onset of old age but also her regard for the virtue of continuing obedience:

> Getting older by the minute,
> Trying not to die;
> 'Fraid of fire and being in it,
> Trusting God Most High!

> I must obey, do what I'm told
> And not just what I like:
> Especially now that I'm old
> And to the grave must hike.

As the community gained stability both within and without, Sister Wilhelmina began experiencing physical precariousness in things which were ordinarily easy, such as experiencing a good night's sleep:

> Give me, Lord, the gift of sleep,
> All my pride away to sweep,
> No more piles of sin to heap,
> Never looking at the cheap
> Baubles that lead to the deep
> Where the hellish sewers seep
> And the smelly demons creep.

This converted poor black sheep
Would into Thine arms now leap
Safe with Thee, with Thee to weep,
And no longer evils reap,
Happy to Thy wishes keep,
With Thee on the mountain steep.
Give me, Lord, the gift of sleep.

On nights when attempts to sleep were futile, sisters would still hear the movement of Sister Wilhelmina's rosary beads in bed. She would sometimes awaken in the night, burning with some inspiration for a new poem, but would still obediently persist in the quest for sleep. Even when she was sleep deprived, nothing seemed to overcome Sister Wilhelmina's characteristic wit and sense of humor. Poems, rhymes, and ditties flowed from her pen, filling a sizeable stack of notebooks. She frequently rewrote the lyrics of familiar songs to be performed at community recreations, with imaginative costumes and dramatic acting. She also composed rhymes to dramatize the little triumphs of daily life:

What joy to know the secret
of unplugging a clogged drain!
What joy no longer to endure
the "call the plumber" pain!
Just baking soda packed in well
and plenty vinegar dosed
Immediately loosens
what was keeping that drain closed.
Let sit for minutes, nine or ten,
then let the water run!

Use plunger to bring up
whatever keeps the job undone.

Sister recognized everything as a gift from the Lord. When anyone asked how she was doing, she would customarily reply, "Grateful to God!" Evidence of this gratitude was her joy that overflowed one Easter morning as she was drying dishes in the kitchen. A sunbeam poured through the chapel window into the main room, prompting Sister Wilhelmina to pause in her work and spontaneously perform a little tap dance routine, probably a remnant from her childhood, in the pool of sunlight, swinging her dishrag. This accomplished, she turned to find a delighted postulant watching her and giggled to see that her little demonstration of joy had been observed.

On one trip, the sisters pulled off at a rest stop at the same time as a busload of African-American women, beautifully dressed, and all wearing long skirts. Seeing them, Sister Wilhelmina began an improvised song to her sisters: "Hooray for the modest ladies, hooray for the modest ladies!" On her way back to the car, some of the group crossed paths with Sister Wilhelmina. Facing the little figure in full habit, bent over her cane, one of the women loudly remarked to another, "Isn't she cute?" At the same volume, Sister Wilhelmina replied earnestly, "I don't mean to be cute!" She turned and then glanced back at them over her shoulder with a smile, pointing her finger over her lifted cane: "I mean to be good!" Whereupon the women all cheered and laughed.

Evidence of the humorous but also determined and meticulous way with which she approached her work is "The

Boulour Book," the booklet that she wrote by hand, "lovingly dedicated to the Postulants of Oblates of Mary, Queen of Apostles," on how to iron the monastic wimple.

> Consider first what you are working with: an iron, a board and your two hands. The iron, usually held in the right hand, can do toe-dancing, drag back on its heel, and do side curving. Occasionally it stamps flat. . . . First of all, there is the preliminary step. Never, never skip this preliminary step. . . . Look at the <u>front</u> of the boulour to see if it is spotlessly clean. Don't bother to iron a stained boulour. Why waste time? No Sister will wear a stained boulour. Simply shove that boulour under the bottom of the pile. . . . I do not recommend leaving unattended boulours on any ironing boards, especially if there are worldly-wise wayfarers tramping through the area solely intent on their own concerns.

She continued to use her simple, monotonous tasks to fuel her spiritual apostolate of prayer, especially prayer for priests. It is evident what mundane chore inspired the following prayer for fallen priests:

> Like wax stuck on a cassock, Lord,
> Are priests in mortal sin!
> Have mercy on them, Jesus!
> Don't let the devil win!
> He's making fun of them and pointing
> At the Church's shame;

Have mercy, Lord! Convert them
For the glory of Thy Name.

With her love of words, she pioneered the use of acrostics in prayer; the hidden word in the following acrostic illustrates the intensity and urgency that she brought to her spiritual apostolate:

Queen Mother Mary—stand with her beside
the cross.
Unite with Mary's slaves, give yourself to her
entirely.
I must be forgotten; exchange it for thou.
Cross is temporary; eternity is forever.
King is Christ; reign with Him at the right
hand of the Father.

In another way, as she reflected on the name of someone in need of prayer, she would use the letters of his name to spell out her own prayer. A classic case is her prayer for the conversion of President Barack Obama:

Obedience to God's law is not optional.
Be born! Believe and be baptized.
Advance and adore Our Lord in the Most
Blessed Sacrament.
Meet Mary the Mother of God. Bring Muslims with you to respond to the miracle she
performs for you.
Admire all saints.

Again and again in her writing, Sister Wilhelmina returned to the idea of the "All-or-Nothing Game." She played this game with many variations, sometimes considering God as "all" and she as "nothing:"

> God always was,
> Will always be,
> Always remains the same;
> He plays with us
> Who live on earth
> His All-or-Nothing game.

> For God is All,
> And we are naught
> Except to pass the test:
> Of choosing
> Between God and men
> Which of them is best.

> For He is All,
> And we are naught,
> Him only we adore;
> No greater good
> Can e'er be sought;
> Let's love Him more and more!

Another variation expresses the "all" that we must give to God and the "nothing" we must keep for ourselves:

> We must give all we have and are,
> With heart, soul, mind and strength;
> Or selfishly live in our sins,
> Until life ends, at length.

Once we have given all to Him,
God joins us to Himself;
If not, we burn for self alone,
On our own pantry shelf.

15

In Gower for Good

In 2010, Sister Wilhelmina was already eighty-six years old. She would still help with the laundry, and she was even known, on occasion, to don her blue work habit and sweep out the barn. Her favorite duty of her elderly years was the care of the priests' ordination cards; each morning she would hang a priest's ordination card at the foot of the crucifix in the chapter room, a sign for the sisters to offer their prayers and sacrifices of the day particularly for that priest. She meticulously recorded the name of the priest in a notebook and kept the collection of cards in perfect alphabetical order.

As age began to prevent her from helping with household duties, she maintained her spiritual apostolate of prayer, primarily through her favorite devotion, the Most Holy Rosary. She would lavish her free time on the Rosary, praying the mysteries, or composing sets of meditations with which to say the Rosary, or writing poems about the Rosary.

God asks that we believe and pray,
And penance do for sin:
Saying the Rosary each day
'Til Heaven we are in!

For reign of Mary's heart we pray
Beside that of her Son;
She stood beside His Cross when man–
Kind's liberty was won.
When Mary reigns, God will be served,
All sodomy will cease!
All men will pray the Rosary
And mankind will have peace.

Sister Wilhelmina's fervent prayer for priests only increased as she entered the most contemplative stage of her life. One sister recounted that "her deep love for priests was very evident, with her heart in her eyes! She was all attention to them when they spoke to her, and was deeply concerned about straying priests or struggling seminarians when such prayer requests were conveyed to her."

Her perception of priests seemed almost prophetic at times. In the early days, before the community had secured a regular chaplain, the sisters occasionally went to a parish near their home for confession. Sister Wilhelmina came out of the church assisted by a sister, where she encountered a young priest whom she had never met. She immediately went into something of a sermon to the priest there on the sidewalk, saying to him, "I am telling you Father, you are God's man," and urged him to be very faithful to his calling. She spoke with such energy that her companion tried to quiet her. It turned out that the priest abandoned his vocation within the year.

Sister loved receiving the first blessings of newly ordained priests in particular. It is an ancient custom to venerate the newly consecrated hands of a new priest by giving a "liturgical kiss" to each hand, a simple and silent gesture after the blessing. Sister Wilhelmina, on the other hand, would loudly give a smacking kiss to each of their hands and in a loud stage whisper say "God bless you!" to the young priest. She would then enthusiastically congratulate the new priest again outside the chapel. She was "all smiles and so full of love and attention to anything they might say," said one sister.

Being elderly did not mean that Sister Wilhelmina lost her sense of fun. She devised names and games for the most mundane of her geriatric equipment: her faithful walker was dubbed Speedy. When a sister came to escort her to Holy Mass, Sister Wilhelmina would grab Speedy's handles and set off with the cry, "Run! Run! Run to Heaven fun!" while the younger sister hastily tried to check the energy of her elderly charge. When Sister Wilhelmina's chronic lung problems required her to use oxygen, she named her portable oxygen tanks Snuff and Puff; and the series of air compressors to fill them were successively Father Air, Uncle Ben, Aunt Jemima, and finally, Cousin Pete.

The respiratory difficulties Sister suffered in later years often resulted in long coughing spells. It was for this reason that Sister was not included in the community's first CDs, according to Sister Therese's decision. This was upheld as future recording sessions became more taxing, due to a contract with Decca Records/de Montfort music. Distributing the music on a larger scale helped defray the construction debt Mother Cecilia had inherited and went on to finance further construction projects. Eventually, the community returned to private productions, and Mother Cecilia saw no reason why Sister Wilhelmina could not be included on at least one of the tracks. So Sister Wilhelmina made her recording debut on *Caroling At Ephesus*, aiding the sisters in recording the final track, "Adeste Fideles." In preparing the piece, her eyes were riveted on Mother Cecilia, who gave her instruction. This, as well as similar instances, reminded Mother Cecilia of the passage in the psalm: "As the eyes of the handmaid are upon the hand of her mistress, so are our eyes turned unto the Lord until He showeth us mercy." Her obedience to Mother Cecilia—fifty-four years her junior— was unwavering, believing she held Christ's place.

All the same, Sister Wilhelmina loved to sing, and she never lost her strong singing voice. Her singing and acting came out uproariously well in a little homemade video, "Elderly," in which she and another sister sang Lerner and Loewe's tune "Wouldn't It Be Loverly" with changed words adapted to describe Sister Wilhelmina's daily life. She was a "ham" and brought much laughter to her sisters, both in production and in the final product.

When her favorite hymns were sung at Mass, such as "O Sacrum Convivium," her dramatic and operatic tone would lead the soprano section, and very frequently completely drown them out, completely oblivious that all the sisters had dissolved into smothered giggles. At recreation, she would regale the sisters and also visitors with her "Negro spirituals."

Sister Wilhelmina also remained in touch with some of her siblings' children, and was always delighted by their visits. One year toward the end of Sister Wilhelmina's life, she received a visit from three of her nieces, the daughters of her sister Christine. The spirituals came out again, and she entertained them with the collection of jokes that she had learned from the novices. "Why was six afraid of seven?" she asked her nonplussed listeners. "You don't know?" Then in triumph she gave the answer, "Because seven ate nine!"

"And how do you catch a unique rabbit?" Again, her question was met with mystified expressions. "You 'neak up on him!" When the laughter subsided, she had a quick follow-up, "And how do you catch a tame rabbit? The tame way!" Her deadpan delivery was also devastating. "I met a bum on the street who said to me, 'I haven't had a bite in weeks.'" "What did you do, Sister Wilhelmina?"

"I bit him."

Yet one more blessing came as the community approached its fourth anniversary in Gower. The Bendictines of Mary received approval of their constitutions in Rome, thanks to Bishop Finn and through the instrumentality of Fr. John Berg. He had urged Mother Cecilia to go to Rome at the funeral of their late friend, Fr. Kenneth Walker. The community had been permitted to make perpetual vows in 2010 so as not to be obliged to keep renewing their private vows, and it was at that ceremony that Sister Wilhelmina received her old ring again, which was newly plated in gold. But the vows were to remain private, and official recognition withheld, as authorities had foreseen an approaching change in community leadership.

Now that stability had been attained, the order she had founded was granted formal ecclesiastical status. On December 8, 2014, Sister Wilhelmina, who was beaming ear to ear, presented the chart solemnizing her vows to Mother Cecilia in the presence of Bishop Finn. The religious vows she had been obliged to sacrifice in taking up private vows in her new community were now fully and wholeheartedly recognized by her beloved Holy Mother, the Church.

16

Looking through the Lattices

As the burdens of old age increased, Sister Wilhelmina received the assistance of "angels," novitiate companions who would help her throughout the day. Paradoxically, the angels were the main beneficiaries of this arrangement, for they witnessed firsthand a faithful religious living her consecration unto the very end. One remarked, "Sr. Wilhelmina makes everything that she does a prayer." The novice mistress, Sister Scholastica, attested to Sister Wilhelmina's fulfilling of the role as the "real novice mistress," as she taught the novices by example how to truly live the religious spirit with complete generosity of heart. One day, Sister Scholastica went as a substitute "angel" for one of her charges who was called away. The last thing to be done in preparing Sister for bed was to administer eye drops. "Now the trick is to get it in the eye, and not down the cheek," she would say to her angels. Sister Scholastica looked for the eye drop box on the shelf but could not find it. Apologizing to Sister Wilhelmina, Sister replied in her funniest tone, "Oh,

121

you're one of those innocent creatures that doesn't know! They put it in an orange bottle now," and there were the eye drops out of sight, tucked inside of a prescription bottle.

All the "angels" testified to Sister Wilhelmina's ability to endure everything without complaint. She would make light of mishaps, a dropped item or something forgotten, with a little jingle like "whoopsie-doopsie-dumsy-dum!" She would even make the best of situations, such as when the water was shut off during construction. Going to the faucet and finding it did not work, she said to her companion with great joy: "Now we can be like the Christ Child and be really poor!"

Her efforts to hide her discomforts made "angeling" a difficult task at times. When Sister Wilhelmina once winced in pain, a novice asked her what was wrong. "Well, I would really like my rosary." The novice persisted. She answered, "See my rosary over there? If I could just have it, I will be fine." "Sister, is it your stomach? I won't give you your rosary unless you tell me." "But if I just put my rosary on it, like this," and she spread her hands over her lap, "everything will be just fine." The novice relented, laughingly saying, "Sister, you are a stinker!" Sister Wilhelmina laughed back and held her rosary close. "Hee-hee . . . yeah, a stinker!"

As surely as her complaining was absent, her compliments were frequent and sincere. "What a nice job you did making that bed!" she would exclaim with gratitude over deeds of service done.

Sister Wilhelmina's strong will certainly found it difficult to be absent from more and more community exercises and to take additional exceptions required by her age. A note of exasperation is found in one of her copybooks, but sublimated into her longing for God and heaven:

"Aren't you tired?" I'm continually asked. Here's my answer:

> I never tire
> Of loving God
> Although I'm
> Surely dying;
> Now that I'm
> Nearly under sod
> It's home to heav'n
> I'm flying.

Whatever it cost her, Sister Wilhelmina resolutely set herself to accept all exceptions as God's will for her and another means of offering Him love and sacrifice. It was a particular cross for her to have to take a snack:

Snack-Time

> For love of God
> I eat this snack,
> Although I'm old
> And dumb and black.
>
> My God is wise,
> He lives in me,
> He does devise
> This poetry.

The daily nap was also difficult for her, but she always accepted in the spirit of obedience:

Obey and Nap

May napping never interfere
With my persistent constant prayer!

I love Thee, Lord, for Thou art here,
Deep in my heart and ev'rywhere!

To the directions of her novitiate angels, so many decades junior to her in both age and religious life, she would constantly reply, "Whatever you say, I will obey."

A particular gift in the final years of Sister Wilhelmina's life was the entrance of a young woman from Kenya. More than twenty years after she had "willingly put beneath her feet all ethnic ties," and "surrendered all attachment to her ethnic origin," her loving Lord gave her another Black sister. On the day of the Kenyan sister's arrival, when she was introduced to Sister Wilhelmina at recreation, Sister Wilhelmina took the young, dark hand with both of hers and would not let it go, stroking it gently and observing now and then with gentle reproach, "Your hands are cold!"

When this sister was preparing to receive the habit and her religious name the following year, Mother Cecilia remembered Sister Wilhelmina's great desire to receive the name of the Precursor of Christ at her own investiture, and so asked Sister Wilhelmina, "Don't you think we need a sister named after St. John the Baptist?" "Oh, yes!" was the enthusiastic reply. When the sister came to greet Sister Wilhelmina after the ceremony, newly named for the Baptist, and with her black face beaming in radiant contrast to her bright new veil, Sister Wilhelmina spread out her arms to embrace her, exclaiming, "I have been waiting for this hug all day!"

The last summer of her life, Sister Wilhelmina was seated outside on the lawn after the first Masses of two newly ordained fraternity priests, Fr. Martin Adams and Fr. Michael Cunningham. An impromptu concert began, with a couple of seminarians fiddling and strumming guitar and banjo. They started playing her favorites, "Deep River," "Swing Low, Sweet Chariot," and "Joshua Fit the Battle of Jericho" for everyone to sing along. After all had joined in for the rousing chorus of "Joshua," the accompanists subsided to simple strumming again, but Sister Wilhelmina recognized her cue. With her unerring sense of rhythm, she launched into a full-throated Gospel solo: "Well, you can talk about the people of Gideon, talk about a man named Saul . . ." She took down the house.

This same summer 2018, on the 4th of July, The community received news that abbatial status was conferred upon them by Rome. Mother Cecilia would be the first Benedictine abbess to receive the traditional blessing in American history. The ceremony took place the day after the consecration of the newly-built abbatial church.

The winter of 2018–2019 saw increasing weakness in Sister Wilhelmina. As the community watched her gradual decline, one of her angels from the novitiate prayed particularly for a preparatory grace before Sister Wilhelmina's passing. The novice's prayer was answered when, on the morning of January 10, she went into Sister Wilhelmina's cell to find her smiling radiantly with "a very pure and innocent expression." "Jesus, Jesus!" Sister Wilhelmina exclaimed, "He is the Good Shepherd. He wants everyone to go to heaven! He says everyone is supposed to go to heaven!"

When asked if she had seen the Lord, she answered, "Yes, I saw Jesus! Everyone in the world, everyone should go to heaven. Heaven, heaven, I want to go to heaven!" She looked up and smiled again, and then turned her eyes to her profession crucifix and gazed at it a long time. To the novice's query, Sister Wilhelmina replied, "Yes, I look at the cross. We should meditate every day on the cross, every single day. We should meditate about His passion. . . . He wants everyone to go to heaven, Oh, how I want to go to heaven!"

She continued to speak animatedly with the novice, in marked contrast to the preceding months in which she had shown increasing difficulty in speech. They spoke first about the necessity of the cross: "It is the right thing to do, you should embrace your cross." And then they spoke about consoling Our Lord: "That is right, it is like entering into eternity." She spoke with the voice of experience, having suffered so much in her religious life, but always embracing that suffering as a means of drawing closer to her beloved Jesus and relieving His thirst for love.

Always faithful to her spiritual motherhood, Sister Wilhelmina promised to pray for the novice, marveling, "You are so young, and I am ancient in comparison to you. I wonder why God kept me so long on earth. Maybe that I tell you all this. . . . We should always love our sisters." She paused and then continued, "And our priests. We should love, always love our holy sisters and our holy priests." She declared, "I want to thank God and praise Him for what He has done for me, I want to thank Him for what He has done for you and I want to thank Him for all He has done for all my Sisters."

A few days after this conversation, these thoughts returned as Sister Wilhelmina was again gazing at the cross: "I'm thinking how Our Lord suffered for us on this cross! I want to pray for the dying! Do you know when I will go to heaven? When will I go to heaven?" Then she exclaimed, "I really want to go to heaven!"

Though this was the clearest and closest event to her death, it was one of the final links in a chain of many other manifestations of the divine in Sister Wilhelmina's life. The most common seemed to be when she was awakening from sleep. One novice, who had had difficulty helping her into bed on account of Sister Wilhelmina's back pain, returned to awaken her. Finding her particularly radiant, the novice said, "Sister, did you see the Blessed Mother?" "Uh-huh!" "Did she speak to you?" "Uh-huh!" "What did she say?" "She said . . ." Sister Wilhelmina caught herself and turned away smiling. When she was told it was time to prepare for Mass, "she ripped out of the chair," as though she were in no pain at all.

On another occasion close to Sister's death, a novice found her awakening very agitated, murmuring something to the effect that she had been witnessing a portion of Our Lord's passion. "They hit Him! They hit Him!" But when fully awake, she would not comment further.

To Mother Abbess Cecilia, again so many years younger in age and religious life, Sister Wilhelmina gave a truly filial trust and obedience. One evening, when Sister Wilhelmina was exhausted from the efforts to prepare for bed and struggling with mounting agitation, the novitiate angels called for Mother Abbess to calm her. As Mother Abbess bent over the elderly sister lying in bed, the abbatial cross around her neck swung forward, and Sister Wilhelmina grasped it tightly in her hands. "Now do you know who I am?" Mother Abbess gently asked her spiritual daughter with a smile. "You're my mother!" came the immediate and happy reply.

In the next few months, Sister Wilhelmina celebrated two significant milestones: on March 9, seventy-five years in vows, and on April 13, ninety-five years of age. On the great occasion of her diamond jubilee, the sisters brought her into the choir before the sanctuary of the abbey church; there she sat, with a gentle smile radiating from her face, while the entire community chanted the *Te Deum* in thanksgiving for the gift of Sister Wilhelmina's religious life.

Difficult goodbyes followed that month as the first daughterhouse of the abbey was made in Ava, Missouri. The founding group was led by Sister Mary Josefa, for whom Sister Wilhelmina had prayed especially since her entrance, and Sister Maria Battista. As the foundresses bade farewell to their original foundress on Mercy Sunday, one of them noticed that Sister did not seem particularly sad. She acted as though she would see them again quite soon, and even said, "I am going with you to Ava."

17

My Home Is over Jordan

During the spring months, Sister Wilhelmina spoke very little and slept more and more. She became completely unresponsive in the afternoon of May 26, which was only the second day in all her elderly years that she was unable to get out of bed. Her last "meal" was her favorite: a couple of spoonfuls of homemade vanilla ice cream. She then received the Last Rites in the morning before the community's Mass.

Her nurse came that evening to do a thorough examination, concluding that Sister Wilhelmina had no more than twenty-four hours to live. Sisters stayed in turns at her bedside that night, beginning the prayers for the dying.

On Monday, May 27, Sister Wilhelmina received not only the Apostolic Blessing but also first blessings from two newly ordained priests. At one point, the community was gathered around her in prayer, when she held her rosary high, gently waving it. Mother Abbess enjoined that the rosary be begun again.

During the conventual Mass, Mother Abbess stayed with

her, and just as the bells for the consecration rang, she witnessed Sister Wilhelmina extend her arms and moan deeply, as though she, in her frail body, were participating in the sacrifice of Our Lord on the cross, taking place in the abbey church just across the courtyard from her room.

Over and over, sisters whispered into her ear the prayer that her mother had taught to her in her early years:

> Jesus, Mary and Joseph I give you my heart
>   and my soul;
> Jesus, Mary, and Joseph, assist me in my last
>   agony.
> Jesus, Mary and Joseph may I breathe forth
>   my spirit
> in peace with you. Amen.

Later that day, the sisters who had moved to Ava, Missouri, exactly one month before to found the abbey's first daughterhouse, returned to say farewell to their beloved sister. All of the Benedictines of Mary, consequently, were present that evening at Sister Wilhelmina's bedside. They recited Matins together in her room before midnight. At least five or six sisters remained praying at her bedside all night, with many others dozing off right in the room or nearby in the hallway outside. Sister Wilhelmina persevered through the entire night, though her breathing was becoming more labored.

On Tuesday morning, May 28, one of the newly ordained priests, Fr. Daniel Powers, FSSP, offered Mass in her room, the fourth Mass of his priesthood. He gave a brief but meaningful sermon on the rewards of heaven: the heavenly crown for which the faithful strive is a reward for charity and is itself an increased capacity for charity. Faithful love of God and neighbor practiced in this earthly life, persevering even until death, opens the soul to share more abundantly in God's life, which is love, in heaven. The dying sister remained unresponsive during this Mass, simply maintaining her struggle to breathe, but the Holy Sacrifice offered next to her and these words about heaven were surely a source of strength.

Sister Wilhelmina continued to be unresponsive until after the conventual Mass, when all the sisters crowded into her cell once again and began singing all of her favorite hymns. Although she did not open her eyes, she obviously could hear the singing, and she even did her best to join in at certain points. Later, the nurse was astonished to hear that Sister Wilhelmina had shown any signs of responsiveness, let alone her attempts to sing, since her blood pressure and oxygen levels normally would have precluded such exertion.

While the sisters were singing, Sister Wilhelmina uttered, or rather sang, her final words, "O Maria," during one of her favorite hymns: "Hail, Holy Queen Enthroned Above." During the singing, her eyes never opened, and her face remained expressionless as she struggled to breathe and even to sing. A few minutes after her final words, however, as the sisters sang "Jesus, My Lord, My God, My All," Sister Wilhelmina's face changed dramatically. While her eyes remained closed, a heavenly smile passed over her face at the words, "Oh with what bursts of fervent praise, Thy goodness, Jesus, would I sing," as though she were granted a vision of the eternity awaiting her, where she would sing His praises forever. This radiant smile shown from her face for the rest of the verse. After about a half hour of singing,

Sister Wilhelmina returned to her unresponsive state and remained so until the next day.

The next day, Wednesday, May 29, the Vigil of the Ascension, after the morning hours of the Divine Office, the sisters gathered again in Sister Wilhelmina's cell to pray the Rosary. Father Powers and the community's chaplain, Father Laurence Carney, also came to recite the prayers for the dying over her. Because of her extremely labored breathing and low oxygen and blood pressure, everyone expected that she would not survive the morning, but little did anyone know that she was waiting to pass from this life in the same way as did her beloved St. Bede.

Years before, one of her novice angels had asked Sister Wilhelmina who was her favorite Benedictine saint, expecting her to name her patron, St. William the Abbot. To the novice's surprise, however, Sister Wilhelmina replied without hesitation, "St. Bede the Venerable! Because his feast was the day on which I became a Benedictine of Mary." Indeed, it was on the feast of St. Bede, May 27, 1995, that she came to Elmhurst, Pennsylvania, to begin the community; the Benedictines of Mary continue to celebrate this feast as their founding day.

Both sisters and nurse expected that Sister Wilhelmina would take her leave on the calendar date of St. Bede's feast, May 27. But the liturgical feast on which he died was Rogation Wednesday, the Vigil of the Ascension, when he expired peacefully as the evening Offices were being completed. He was consequently considered to have died on the feast of the Ascension, since First Vespers of the feast had been chanted, and it was an hour after sunset. Sister Wilhelmina would follow in her beloved saint's footsteps, not only in his love of the Divine Office and our Blessed Lady, but even in his manner of death.

The afternoon of May 29, just after a sister brought the Pilgrim Virgin statue from Fatima into Sister Wilhelmina's cell, Mother Abbess was inspired to dress Sister Wilhelmina in the habit once again as best as could be done, remembering how great was Sister Wilhelmina's desire to die wearing it. Later, the sisters realized the uncanny parallel to the time when Sister Wilhelmina had reassumed the traditional habit in 1974, on the occasion of the pilgrim statue's visit to the Oblate Sisters of Providence.

The feast of the Ascension had begun with First Vespers, and the whole community assembled at 7:00 p.m. in Sister Wilhelmina's cell where Mother Abbess read aloud numerous messages of assurance of prayers, along with prayer requests from family and friends. During the reading, Sister Wilhelmina remained unresponsive, but there can be little doubt that she took everything to heart as she lay there, clutching her profession crucifix and her well-used rosary. The whole community experienced a certain joy and peace for the first time at these oft-repeated gatherings around her bed.

After singing some more of Sister Wilhelmina's favorite hymns to Our Lady, the community chanted Compline together in her cell. Compline concludes with the ancient custom of the superior giving the community a blessing with holy water for the night. Mother Abbess intoned the customary antiphon for Paschaltide:

Vidi aquam egredientem de templo, a latere
dextro, alleluia:
Et omnes ad quos pervenit aqua ista, salvi facti
sunt, et dicent: alleluia, alleluia.

I saw water flowing out of the Temple, from
its right side, Alleluia:
And all who came to this water were saved,
And they shall say: Alleluia, Alleluia.

As the sisters continued the antiphon, Mother Abbess froze, her eyes fixed upon Sister Wilhelmina, who had suddenly taken on an air of profound peace. Intuitively, after Mother Abbess blessed herself with holy water, she sprinkled Sister Wilhelmina's head, then sprinkled her again more copiously, signing a cross upon Sister Wilhelmina's forehead with her thumb in the water, "as if she were baptizing her again," as one sister later commented. Mother Abbess gently stroked her cheeks, and as she withdrew her hand (but not her gaze) to continue blessing the rest of the community, Sister Wilhelmina breathed her last, peacefully and without a struggle.

The moment of Sister Wilhelmina's death corresponded exactly with the antiphon, for she received holy water from the right hand of her successor, who had been blessed as the community's first abbess less than nine months before, whom Sister Wilhelmina ardently venerated as Christ Himself. Sister Wilhelmina received the water from the temple of the Lord's pierced Heart, which was symbolized by the abbey church, and she died in the shadow of this edifice, which had also been consecrated less than nine months before. Ninety-five years after receiving the saving water of Baptism on May 30, 1924, Sister Wilhelmina's passing on May 29, 2019, consummated her religious vows which were her "second baptism." She took her flight to God, following the Lord in the mystery of His wonderful ascension, as the community would sing in the Mass of the Ascension the following day. It was through the veil of this life that she was able to complete the antiphon and testify to the water through which she and the saints of Christ are saved, to sing "Alleluia" to her Bridegroom forever.

Spontaneously, Mother Abbess knelt at Sister Wilhelmina's side after blessing the sisters, and all the sisters knelt also as Mother Abbess gently said, "She's gone." Mother Abbess began to weep, saying, "Oh, Sister, Sister, pray for us," as she kissed the limp hand and, in an eloquent gesture, took Sister Wilhelmina's thumb to trace the sign of the cross upon her own forehead, receiving the blessing of her predecessor and foundress, even as Sister Wilhelmina had not departed without receiving the blessing of her new Mother Abbess.

Mother Abbess wept again and, overwhelmed with gratitude that all the sisters had together witnessed such a grace, cried out, "How much God loves us! How much He loves our community!" Our Lord could not have chosen a more fitting nor consoling moment to withdraw the treasure of the community unto Himself. The sisters also wept, but the tears were more of joy than of grief. One sister recalled seeing Sister Scholastica, smiling through her tears just after the passing, whispering, "Well done, well done!" Yet another sister, who tends to be more reserved, actually let out a chuckle, as she thought, "You little stinker, slipping off to heaven just like that!" Sister Wilhelmina would have undoubtedly answered her, "Hee-hee . . . yeah, a stinker!" Sisters collected their rosaries they had twined around her hands, brushed away their tears, and lovingly took up their choir books to sing the "Subvenite," the song of departure. As the mellow tones of the traditional prayer for a deceased community member wafted heavenward, the church bell tolled ninety-five times, commemorating the many years of Sister Wilhelmina's rich and holy life.

Our loving Lord had seen to it that the entire community was present to witness the holy death of their foundress, after completing the final Office of the day, and the final Office of Sister Wilhelmina's long and venerable life.

Mother Abbess clothed Sister Wilhelmina with her cuculla, the garment of her monastic profession, crowned her with flowers and placed the chart of her solemn profession at her feet. Sisters then took turns keeping watch by the hour as Sister Wilhelmina lay in state in the chapterhouse. They continuously prayed the Psalms for the Dead until Friday morning, when a sunbeam poured in through the chapterhouse window and robed Sister Wilhelmina's little body in glory, leaving the shadow of a cross at her feet. Sisters remarked on the beauty that she assumed, as she seemed to smile more and more until the coffin, handmade by Fr. Joseph Terra, FSSP, was closed and her beautiful face could no longer be seen.

Fr. Arnaud Devillers, with whom Sister Wilhelmina had founded the community in 1995, offered her funeral Mass. Following the Mass, he remarked that of the many sisters he had met, he had full confidence in Sister Wilhelmina's genuineness because of her humility. It was upon that foundation that a new community arose for the glory of God.

After the funeral Mass, the sisters carried their beloved foundress to the abbey cemetery, in which earlier that morning they had dug by hand its first grave. After the fathers and brothers of several of the sisters lowered the little coffin into the ground, the sisters, relatives, and friends of Sister Wilhelmina passed one by one to shovel some earth into the grave. The sorrow of the parting made many tears flow, but all experienced a deep peace and hope. The little body that they had laid to rest was like the husk of a precious seed that would continue to bear fruit unto eternal life.

Later at the reception, one of Sister Wilhelmina's nieces commented in surprise at the number of people in attendance; she asked if Sister Wilhelmina's funeral were coinciding with a family visit for some of the other sisters. "Oh, no," the sisters replied. "All these people came to pay their respects to Sister Wilhelmina." "Well!" Sister Wilhelmina's niece remarked. "I didn't know her tribe was so big!"

Giving Thanks

Indeed, Sister Wilhelmina's "tribe" is very big, and grows more so with each passing day. Sister Wilhelmina touched many lives in the course of her ninety-five years, and even now, her sisters, relatives, and friends continue to turn to her as a source of inspiration and even of intercessory prayer.

Soon after Sister Wilhelmina's death, one of the sisters' nephews, a two-year-old boy, got into a bottle of Tylenol and consumed most of it by the time he was discovered. His distraught mother brought him to the hospital and feared him to be dying. The doctors concurred likewise, and flew him to a larger hospital after administering emergency treatment. Liver failure was projected, and his chance of survival was extremely slim. The sister immediately enlisted Sister Wilhelmina's help and encouraged her other Benedictine sisters to do likewise, asking for the nephew's cure and to avoid any medical measures against the Church's teaching on end-of-life issues. After a harrowing two days, the liver enzymes, which had risen to deadly levels, suddenly subsided, leaving no trace of damage. A family member pronounced it "nothing short of a miracle," and the boy was discharged after a few days. When paying a visit to the abbey, the youngster was encouraged to thank Sister Wilhelmina. He then knelt at her grave and gave her tombstone a big, smacking kiss. He remains a healthy little boy to this day.

Reports of other miracles find their way to the abbey. Some are, like Sister Wilhelmina's life, a drawn-out blessing. A mother of a large family had been suffering terribly for years with a strange reaction to a prescribed medicine. Invoking Sister Wilhelmina, she has found that her strength has gradually been increasing so that she can return to her maternal duties. The family found itself more unified and faith-filled, even though the physical improvement was slow.

Some of the miracles are also like Sister Wilhelmina's life, inconspicuous, but still wonderful. A benefactor who had a chronic ailment touched Sister Wilhelmina's memorial card to herself before retiring, and she awoke without pain.

In another miracle, a sister's blood sister was expecting her third child. She had consecrated her little one to the Blessed Mother in the womb and named him Emmanuel, and had a premonition of future danger. As it turned out, she contracted a very rare infection of the heart. An emergency C-section was done to save the child. The little one was unfortunately lost, but the family began invoking the intercession of Sister Wilhelmina, as the young mother's life was gravely imperiled. Her heart stopped working, and dramatic measures were taken, though her life was still despaired of. Though the lack of circulation caused the loss of her left hand, the young mother defied all expectations and began to rally, and she is on the road to recovery.

Around the time of Sister Wilhelmina's passing, one of the sisters became very ill. Mother Abbess prayed to Sister Wilhelmina asking her, in the true spirit of obedience that she always rendered to her, to obtain the grace of this sister's healing on August 29, the day marking three months since Sister Wilhelmina's death. Mother Abbess also asked all the sisters to pray to Sister Wilhelmina for a special grace without specifying her intention. August 29 came, and the sister remained unwell.

Toward evening, around the same time Sister Wilhelmina had passed on May 29, the sister became violently ill, expelling the infection that had been menacing her for months. When that subsided, she went to the abbey church to pray, asking Sister to ensure her healing in the name of holy obedience, the virtue that Sister Wilhelmina exemplified. Just before she left the church at midnight, she felt a tingling sensation, not at all like the pain that she had been experiencing. She returned to her cell and fell into a deep sleep in which she dreamed that she was looking across the field where Sister Wilhelmina was buried, which was full of beautiful flowers. While she could not actually see her, Sister Wilhelmina stood next to her, and in a voice that "sounded younger," she told the sister that she was cured of her illness, but that she had to be careful of her diet lest she relapse: she must take baking soda for ten days, flax oil, and lots of vegetables. The sister awoke, completely cured. Mother Abbess and all the sisters rejoiced at the sister's healing and that now, after so many years of obedience to the infirmarian and novitiate angels' directions, Sister Wilhelmina could now give instructions to her sisters. Mother Abbess Cecilia led the community in a Rosary procession of thanksgiving.

Mother Abbess addressed the community, exhorting all the sisters to show their gratitude through generosity:

> God is good to us! He wants to give us more than we could possibly imagine. We simply have to have greater faith, and the whole canopy of heaven is opened to us. Our dear Sr. Wilhelmina is a saint in heaven! How blessed we are. We can never, never forget how much He has blessed us in so many ways. So let's be generous with Him, and hold nothing back—especially the amount of faith in our hearts, and absolute confident trust in His mercy and tenderness towards us. And just as important, our loving obedience to His will, manifested by our superiors and the circumstances around us, following the beautiful example of dear Sister.

↜

If there is anything I would want to pass on to the community, it would be this: Devotion to Our Blessed Mother. True Devotion to Our Blessed Mother.

—Sister Wilhelmina in her final years